Python 3.5 Setup and Usage Guide

A catalogue record for this book is available from the Hong Kong Public Libraries.

Published by Samurai Media Limited.

Email: info@samuraimedia.org

ISBN 978-988-14436-7-0

Contents

This part of the documentation is devoted to general information on the setup of the Python environment on different platform, the invocation of the interpreter and things that make working with Python easier.

CONTENTS

COMMAND LINE AND ENVIRONMENT

The CPython interpreter scans the command line and the environment for various settings.

CPython implementation detail: Other implementations' command line schemes may differ. See *implementations* for further resources.

1.1 Command line

When invoking Python, you may specify any of these options:

```
python [ bBdEhiIOqsSuvVWx?] [ c command | m module name | script | ] [args]
```

The most common use case is, of course, a simple invocation of a script:

```
python myscript.py
```

1.1.1 Interface options

The interpreter interface resembles that of the UNIX shell, but provides some additional methods of invocation:

- When called with standard input connected to a tty device, it prompts for commands and executes them until an EOF (an end-of-file character, you can produce that with *Ctrl-D* on UNIX or *Ctrl-Z, Enter* on Windows) is read.

- When called with a file name argument or with a file as standard input, it reads and executes a script from that file.

- When called with a directory name argument, it reads and executes an appropriately named script from that directory.

- When called with -c command, it executes the Python statement(s) given as *command*. Here *command* may contain multiple statements separated by newlines. Leading whitespace is significant in Python statements!

- When called with -m module-name, the given module is located on the Python module path and executed as a script.

In non-interactive mode, the entire input is parsed before it is executed.

An interface option terminates the list of options consumed by the interpreter, all consecutive arguments will end up in sys.argv – note that the first element, subscript zero (sys.argv[0]), is a string reflecting the program's source.

-c <command>
  Execute the Python code in *command*. *command* can be one or more statements separated by newlines, with significant leading whitespace as in normal module code.

  If this option is given, the first element of sys.argv will be "-c" and the current directory will be added to the start of sys.path (allowing modules in that directory to be imported as top level modules).

-m `<module-name>`

Search `sys.path` for the named module and execute its contents as the `__main__` module.

Since the argument is a *module* name, you must not give a file extension (`.py`). The `module-name` should be a valid Python module name, but the implementation may not always enforce this (e.g. it may allow you to use a name that includes a hyphen).

Package names (including namespace packages) are also permitted. When a package name is supplied instead of a normal module, the interpreter will execute `<pkg>.__main__` as the main module. This behaviour is deliberately similar to the handling of directories and zipfiles that are passed to the interpreter as the script argument.

Note: This option cannot be used with built-in modules and extension modules written in C, since they do not have Python module files. However, it can still be used for precompiled modules, even if the original source file is not available.

If this option is given, the first element of `sys.argv` will be the full path to the module file (while the module file is being located, the first element will be set to `"-m"`). As with the `-c` option, the current directory will be added to the start of `sys.path`.

Many standard library modules contain code that is invoked on their execution as a script. An example is the `timeit` module:

```
python -mtimeit -s 'setup here' 'benchmarked code here'
python -mtimeit -h # for details
```

See also:

runpy.run_module() Equivalent functionality directly available to Python code

PEP 338 – Executing modules as scripts

Changed in version 3.1: Supply the package name to run a `__main__` submodule.

Changed in version 3.4: namespace packages are also supported

-

Read commands from standard input (`sys.stdin`). If standard input is a terminal, `-i` is implied.

If this option is given, the first element of `sys.argv` will be `"-"` and the current directory will be added to the start of `sys.path`.

`<script>`

Execute the Python code contained in *script*, which must be a filesystem path (absolute or relative) referring to either a Python file, a directory containing a `__main__.py` file, or a zipfile containing a `__main__.py` file.

If this option is given, the first element of `sys.argv` will be the script name as given on the command line.

If the script name refers directly to a Python file, the directory containing that file is added to the start of `sys.path`, and the file is executed as the `__main__` module.

If the script name refers to a directory or zipfile, the script name is added to the start of `sys.path` and the `__main__.py` file in that location is executed as the `__main__` module.

See also:

runpy.run_path() Equivalent functionality directly available to Python code

---

If no interface option is given, `-i` is implied, `sys.argv[0]` is an empty string (`""`) and the current directory will be added to the start of `sys.path`. Also, tab-completion and history editing is automatically enabled, if available on your platform (see *rlcompleter-config*).

See also:

tut-invoking

Changed in version 3.4: Automatic enabling of tab-completion and history editing.

1.1.2 Generic options

-?
-h
--help
> Print a short description of all command line options.

-V
--version
> Print the Python version number and exit. Example output could be:

```
Python 3.0
```

1.1.3 Miscellaneous options

-b
> Issue a warning when comparing `bytes` or `bytearray` with `str` or `bytes` with `int`. Issue an error when the option is given twice (`-bb`).

-B
> If given, Python won't try to write `.pyc` files on the import of source modules. See also `PYTHONDONTWRITEBYTECODE`.

-d
> Turn on parser debugging output (for wizards only, depending on compilation options). See also `PYTHONDEBUG`.

-E
> Ignore all `PYTHON*` environment variables, e.g. `PYTHONPATH` and `PYTHONHOME`, that might be set.

-i
> When a script is passed as first argument or the `-c` option is used, enter interactive mode after executing the script or the command, even when `sys.stdin` does not appear to be a terminal. The `PYTHONSTARTUP` file is not read.
>
> This can be useful to inspect global variables or a stack trace when a script raises an exception. See also `PYTHONINSPECT`.

-I
> Run Python in isolated mode. This also implies -E and -s. In isolated mode `sys.path` contains neither the script's directory nor the user's site-packages directory. All `PYTHON*` environment variables are ignored, too. Further restrictions may be imposed to prevent the user from injecting malicious code.
>
> New in version 3.4.

-O
> Turn on basic optimizations. This changes the filename extension for compiled (*bytecode*) files from `.pyc` to `.pyo`. See also `PYTHONOPTIMIZE`.

-OO

> Discard docstrings in addition to the $-O$ optimizations.

-q

> Don't display the copyright and version messages even in interactive mode.
>
> New in version 3.2.

-R

> Kept for compatibility. On Python 3.3 and greater, hash randomization is turned on by default.
>
> On previous versions of Python, this option turns on hash randomization, so that the __hash__() values of str, bytes and datetime are "salted" with an unpredictable random value. Although they remain constant within an individual Python process, they are not predictable between repeated invocations of Python.
>
> Hash randomization is intended to provide protection against a denial-of-service caused by carefully-chosen inputs that exploit the worst case performance of a dict construction, O(n^2) complexity. See http://www.ocert.org/advisories/ocert-2011-003.html for details.
>
> PYTHONHASHSEED allows you to set a fixed value for the hash seed secret.
>
> New in version 3.2.3.

-s

> Don't add the user site-packages directory to sys.path.
>
> **See also:**
>
> **PEP 370** – Per user site-packages directory

-S

> Disable the import of the module site and the site-dependent manipulations of sys.path that it entails. Also disable these manipulations if site is explicitly imported later (call site.main() if you want them to be triggered).

-u

> Force the binary layer of the stdout and stderr streams (which is available as their buffer attribute) to be unbuffered. The text I/O layer will still be line-buffered if writing to the console, or block-buffered if redirected to a non-interactive file.
>
> See also PYTHONUNBUFFERED.

-v

> Print a message each time a module is initialized, showing the place (filename or built-in module) from which it is loaded. When given twice ($-vv$), print a message for each file that is checked for when searching for a module. Also provides information on module cleanup at exit. See also PYTHONVERBOSE.

-W arg

> Warning control. Python's warning machinery by default prints warning messages to sys.stderr. A typical warning message has the following form:
>
> ```
> file:line: category: message
> ```
>
> By default, each warning is printed once for each source line where it occurs. This option controls how often warnings are printed.
>
> Multiple $-W$ options may be given; when a warning matches more than one option, the action for the last matching option is performed. Invalid $-W$ options are ignored (though, a warning message is printed about invalid options when the first warning is issued).
>
> Warnings can also be controlled from within a Python program using the warnings module.
>
> The simplest form of argument is one of the following action strings (or a unique abbreviation):

ignore Ignore all warnings.

default Explicitly request the default behavior (printing each warning once per source line).

all Print a warning each time it occurs (this may generate many messages if a warning is triggered repeatedly for the same source line, such as inside a loop).

module Print each warning only the first time it occurs in each module.

once Print each warning only the first time it occurs in the program.

error Raise an exception instead of printing a warning message.

The full form of argument is:

```
action:message:category:module:line
```

Here, *action* is as explained above but only applies to messages that match the remaining fields. Empty fields match all values; trailing empty fields may be omitted. The *message* field matches the start of the warning message printed; this match is case-insensitive. The *category* field matches the warning category. This must be a class name; the match tests whether the actual warning category of the message is a subclass of the specified warning category. The full class name must be given. The *module* field matches the (fully-qualified) module name; this match is case-sensitive. The *line* field matches the line number, where zero matches all line numbers and is thus equivalent to an omitted line number.

See also:

`warnings` the warnings module

PEP 230 – Warning framework

`PYTHONWARNINGS`

-x

Skip the first line of the source, allowing use of non-Unix forms of `#!cmd`. This is intended for a DOS specific hack only.

Note: The line numbers in error messages will be off by one.

-X

Reserved for various implementation-specific options. CPython currently defines the following possible values:

- `-X faulthandler` to enable `faulthandler`;

- `-X showrefcount` to enable the output of the total reference count and memory blocks (only works on debug builds);

- `-X tracemalloc` to start tracing Python memory allocations using the `tracemalloc` module. By default, only the most recent frame is stored in a traceback of a trace. Use `-X tracemalloc=NFRAME` to start tracing with a traceback limit of *NFRAME* frames. See the `tracemalloc.start()` for more information.

It also allows to pass arbitrary values and retrieve them through the `sys._xoptions` dictionary.

Changed in version 3.2: It is now allowed to pass *-X* with CPython.

New in version 3.3: The `-X faulthandler` option.

New in version 3.4: The `-X showrefcount` and `-X tracemalloc` options.

1.1.4 Options you shouldn't use

-J

Reserved for use by Jython.

1.2 Environment variables

These environment variables influence Python's behavior, they are processed before the command-line switches other than -E or -I. It is customary that command-line switches override environmental variables where there is a conflict.

PYTHONHOME

Change the location of the standard Python libraries. By default, the libraries are searched in *prefix*/lib/python*version* and *exec_prefix*/lib/python*version*, where *prefix* and *exec_prefix* are installation-dependent directories, both defaulting to /usr/local.

When PYTHONHOME is set to a single directory, its value replaces both *prefix* and *exec_prefix*. To specify different values for these, set PYTHONHOME to *prefix*:*exec_prefix*.

PYTHONPATH

Augment the default search path for module files. The format is the same as the shell's PATH: one or more directory pathnames separated by os.pathsep (e.g. colons on Unix or semicolons on Windows). Non-existent directories are silently ignored.

In addition to normal directories, individual PYTHONPATH entries may refer to zipfiles containing pure Python modules (in either source or compiled form). Extension modules cannot be imported from zipfiles.

The default search path is installation dependent, but generally begins with *prefix*/lib/python*version* (see PYTHONHOME above). It is *always* appended to PYTHONPATH.

An additional directory will be inserted in the search path in front of PYTHONPATH as described above under *Interface options*. The search path can be manipulated from within a Python program as the variable sys.path.

PYTHONSTARTUP

If this is the name of a readable file, the Python commands in that file are executed before the first prompt is displayed in interactive mode. The file is executed in the same namespace where interactive commands are executed so that objects defined or imported in it can be used without qualification in the interactive session. You can also change the prompts sys.ps1 and sys.ps2 and the hook sys.__interactivehook__ in this file.

PYTHONOPTIMIZE

If this is set to a non-empty string it is equivalent to specifying the $-O$ option. If set to an integer, it is equivalent to specifying $-O$ multiple times.

PYTHONDEBUG

If this is set to a non-empty string it is equivalent to specifying the $-d$ option. If set to an integer, it is equivalent to specifying $-d$ multiple times.

PYTHONINSPECT

If this is set to a non-empty string it is equivalent to specifying the $-i$ option.

This variable can also be modified by Python code using os.environ to force inspect mode on program termination.

PYTHONUNBUFFERED

If this is set to a non-empty string it is equivalent to specifying the $-u$ option.

PYTHONVERBOSE

If this is set to a non-empty string it is equivalent to specifying the $-v$ option. If set to an integer, it is equivalent to specifying $-v$ multiple times.

PYTHONCASEOK

If this is set, Python ignores case in `import` statements. This only works on Windows and OS X.

PYTHONDONTWRITEBYTECODE

If this is set to a non-empty string, Python won't try to write `.pyc` or `.pyo` files on the import of source modules. This is equivalent to specifying the `-B` option.

PYTHONHASHSEED

If this variable is not set or set to `random`, a random value is used to seed the hashes of str, bytes and datetime objects.

If `PYTHONHASHSEED` is set to an integer value, it is used as a fixed seed for generating the hash() of the types covered by the hash randomization.

Its purpose is to allow repeatable hashing, such as for selftests for the interpreter itself, or to allow a cluster of python processes to share hash values.

The integer must be a decimal number in the range [0,4294967295]. Specifying the value 0 will disable hash randomization.

New in version 3.2.3.

PYTHONIOENCODING

If this is set before running the interpreter, it overrides the encoding used for stdin/stdout/stderr, in the syntax `encodingname:errorhandler`. Both the `encodingname` and the `:errorhandler` parts are optional and have the same meaning as in `str.encode()`.

For stderr, the `:errorhandler` part is ignored; the handler will always be `'backslashreplace'`.

Changed in version 3.4: The `encodingname` part is now optional.

PYTHONNOUSERSITE

If this is set, Python won't add the `user site-packages directory` to `sys.path`.

See also:

PEP 370 – Per user site-packages directory

PYTHONUSERBASE

Defines the `user base directory`, which is used to compute the path of the `user site-packages directory` and *Distutils installation paths* for `python setup.py install --user`.

See also:

PEP 370 – Per user site-packages directory

PYTHONEXECUTABLE

If this environment variable is set, `sys.argv[0]` will be set to its value instead of the value got through the C runtime. Only works on Mac OS X.

PYTHONWARNINGS

This is equivalent to the `-W` option. If set to a comma separated string, it is equivalent to specifying `-W` multiple times.

PYTHONFAULTHANDLER

If this environment variable is set to a non-empty string, `faulthandler.enable()` is called at startup: install a handler for `SIGSEGV`, `SIGFPE`, `SIGABRT`, `SIGBUS` and `SIGILL` signals to dump the Python traceback. This is equivalent to `-X faulthandler` option.

New in version 3.3.

PYTHONTRACEMALLOC

If this environment variable is set to a non-empty string, start tracing Python memory allocations using the `tracemalloc` module. The value of the variable is the maximum number of frames stored in a traceback of a trace. For example, `PYTHONTRACEMALLOC=1` stores only the most recent frame. See the `tracemalloc.start()` for more information.

New in version 3.4.

PYTHONASYNCIODEBUG

If this environment variable is set to a non-empty string, enable the *debug mode* of the `asyncio` module.

New in version 3.4.

1.2.1 Debug-mode variables

Setting these variables only has an effect in a debug build of Python, that is, if Python was configured with the `--with-pydebug` build option.

PYTHONTHREADDEBUG

If set, Python will print threading debug info.

PYTHONDUMPREFS

If set, Python will dump objects and reference counts still alive after shutting down the interpreter.

PYTHONMALLOCSTATS

If set, Python will print memory allocation statistics every time a new object arena is created, and on shutdown.

USING PYTHON ON UNIX PLATFORMS

2.1 Getting and installing the latest version of Python

2.1.1 On Linux

Python comes preinstalled on most Linux distributions, and is available as a package on all others. However there are certain features you might want to use that are not available on your distro's package. You can easily compile the latest version of Python from source.

In the event that Python doesn't come preinstalled and isn't in the repositories as well, you can easily make packages for your own distro. Have a look at the following links:

See also:

http://www.debian.org/doc/manuals/maint-guide/first.en.html for Debian users

http://en.opensuse.org/Portal:Packaging for OpenSuse users

http://docs.fedoraproject.org/en-US/Fedora_Draft_Documentation/0.1/html/RPM_Guide/ch-creating-rpms.html for Fedora users

http://www.slackbook.org/html/package-management-making-packages.html for Slackware users

2.1.2 On FreeBSD and OpenBSD

- FreeBSD users, to add the package use:

  ```
  pkg_add -r python
  ```

- OpenBSD users use:

  ```
  pkg_add ftp://ftp.openbsd.org/pub/OpenBSD/4.2/packages/<insert your architecture here>
  ```

  For example i386 users get the 2.5.1 version of Python using:

  ```
  pkg_add ftp://ftp.openbsd.org/pub/OpenBSD/4.2/packages/i386/python-2.5.1p2.tgz
  ```

2.1.3 On OpenSolaris

You can get Python from OpenCSW. Various versions of Python are available and can be installed with e.g. `pkgutil -i python27`.

2.2 Building Python

If you want to compile CPython yourself, first thing you should do is get the source. You can download either the latest release's source or just grab a fresh clone. (If you want to contribute patches, you will need a clone.)

The build process consists in the usual

```
./configure
make
make install
```

invocations. Configuration options and caveats for specific Unix platforms are extensively documented in the README file in the root of the Python source tree.

> **Warning:** make install can overwrite or masquerade the python3 binary. make altinstall is therefore recommended instead of make install since it only installs *exec_prefix*/bin/python*version*.

2.3 Python-related paths and files

These are subject to difference depending on local installation conventions; prefix (${prefix}) and exec_prefix (${exec_prefix}) are installation-dependent and should be interpreted as for GNU software; they may be the same.

For example, on most Linux systems, the default for both is /usr.

File/directory	Meaning
exec_prefix/bin/python3	Recommended location of the interpreter.
prefix/lib/python*version*, *exec_prefix*/lib/python*version*	Recommended locations of the directories containing the standard modules.
prefix/include/python*version*, *exec_prefix*/include/python*versi*	Recommended locations of the directories containing the include files needed for developing Python extensions and embedding the interpreter.

2.4 Miscellaneous

To easily use Python scripts on Unix, you need to make them executable, e.g. with

```
$ chmod +x script
```

and put an appropriate Shebang line at the top of the script. A good choice is usually

```
#!/usr/bin/env python3
```

which searches for the Python interpreter in the whole PATH. However, some Unices may not have the **env** command, so you may need to hardcode /usr/bin/python3 as the interpreter path.

To use shell commands in your Python scripts, look at the subprocess module.

2.5 Editors

Vim and Emacs are excellent editors which support Python very well. For more information on how to code in Python in these editors, look at:

- http://www.vim.org/scripts/script.php?script_id=790

- http://sourceforge.net/projects/python-mode

Geany is an excellent IDE with support for a lot of languages. For more information, read: http://www.geany.org/

Komodo edit is another extremely good IDE. It also has support for a lot of languages. For more information, read http://komodoide.com/.

USING PYTHON ON WINDOWS

This document aims to give an overview of Windows-specific behaviour you should know about when using Python on Microsoft Windows.

3.1 Installing Python

Unlike most Unix systems and services, Windows does not include a system supported installation of Python. To make Python available, the CPython team has compiled Windows installers (MSI packages) with every release for many years. These installers are primarily intended to add a per-user installation of Python, with the core interpreter and library being used by a single user. The installer is also able to install for all users of a single machine, and a separate ZIP file is available for application-local distributions.

3.1.1 Installation Steps

Four Python 3.5 installers are available for download - two each for the 32-bit and 64-bit versions of the interpreter. The *web installer* is a small initial download, and it will automatically download the required components as necessary. The *offline installer* includes the components necessary for a default installation and only requires an internet connection for optional features. See *Installing Without Downloading* for other ways to avoid downloading during installation.

After starting the installer, one of two options may be selected:

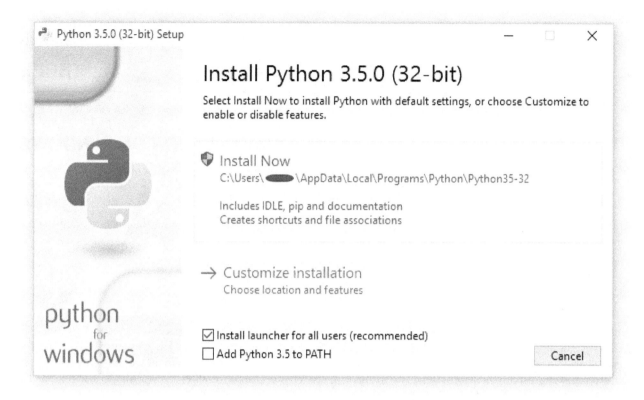

If you select "Install Now":

- You will *not* need to be an administrator (unless a system update for the C Runtime Library is required or you install the *Python Launcher for Windows* for all users)

- Python will be installed into your user directory

- The *Python Launcher for Windows* will be installed according to the option at the bottom of the first pace

- The standard library, test suite, launcher and pip will be installed

- If selected, the install directory will be added to your PATH

- Shortcuts will only be visible for the current user

Selecting "Customize installation" will allow you to select the features to install, the installation location and other options or post-install actions. To install debugging symbols or binaries, you will need to use this option.

To perform an all-users installation, you should select "Customize installation". In this case:

- You may be required to provide administrative credentials or approval

- Python will be installed into the Program Files directory

- The *Python Launcher for Windows* will be installed into the Windows directory

- Optional features may be selected during installation

- The standard library can be pre-compiled to bytecode

- If selected, the install directory will be added to the system PATH

- Shortcuts are available for all users

3.1.2 Installing Without UI

All of the options available in the installer UI can also be specified from the command line, allowing scripted installers to replicate an installation on many machines without user interaction. These options may also be set without suppressing the UI in order to change some of the defaults.

To completely hide the installer UI and install Python silently, pass the `/quiet` (`/q`) option. To skip past the user interaction but still display progress and errors, pass the `/passive` (`/p`) option. The `/uninstall` option may be passed to immediately begin removing Python - no prompt will be displayed.

All other options are passed as `name=value`, where the value is usually `0` to disable a feature, `1` to enable a feature, or a path. The full list of available options is shown below.

Name	Description	Default
InstallAllUsers	Perform a system-wide installation.	1
TargetDir	The installation directory	Selected based on InstallAllUsers
DefaultAllUsersTargetDir	The default installation directory for all-user installs	`%ProgramFiles%\Python X.Y` or `%ProgramFiles(x86)%\Python X.Y`
DefaultJustForMeTargetDir	The default install directory for just-for-me installs	`%LocalAppData%\Programs\PythonXY` or `%LocalAppData%\Programs\PythonXY-32`
DefaultCustomTargetDir	The default custom install directory displayed in the UI	(empty)
AssociateFiles	Create file associations if the launcher is also installed.	1
CompileAll	Compile all `.py` files to `.pyc`.	0
PrependPath	Add install and Scripts directories tho `PATH` and `.PY` to `PATHEXT`	0
Shortcuts	Create shortcuts for the interpreter, documentation and IDLE if installed.	1
Include_doc	Install Python manual	1
Include_debug	Install debug binaries	0
Include_dev	Install developer headers and libraries	1
Include_exe	Install `python.exe` and related files	1
Include_launcher	Install *Python Launcher for Windows*.	1
InstallLauncherAllUsers	Installs *Python Launcher for Windows* for all users.	1
Include_lib	Install standard library and extension modules	1
Include_pip	Install bundled pip and setuptools	1
Include_symbols	Install debugging symbols (*.pdb)	0
Include_tcltk	Install Tcl/Tk support and IDLE	1
Include_test	Install standard library test suite	1
Include_tools	Install utility scripts	1
LauncherOnly	Only installs the launcher. This will override most other options.	0
SimpleInstall	Disable most install UI	0
SimpleInstallDescription	A custom message to display when the simplified install UI is used.	(empty)

For example, to silently install a default, system-wide Python installation, you could use the following command (from an elevated command prompt):

```
python-3.5.0.exe /quiet InstallAllUsers=1 PrependPath=1 Include_test=0
```

To allow users to easily install a personal copy of Python without the test suite, you could provide a shortcut with the following command. This will display a simplified initial page and disallow customization:

```
python-3.5.0.exe InstallAllUsers=0 Include_launcher=0 Include_test=0
    SimpleInstall=1 SimpleInstallDescription="Just for me, no test suite."
```

(Note that omitting the launcher also omits file associations, and is only recommended for per-user installs when there is also a system-wide installation that included the launcher.)

The options listed above can also be provided in a file named `unattend.xml` alongside the executable. This file specifies a list of options and values. When a value is provided as an attribute, it will be converted to a number if possible. Values provided as element text are always left as strings. This example file sets the same options and the previous example:

```
<Options>
    <Option Name="InstallAllUsers" Value="no" />
    <Option Name="Include_launcher" Value="0" />
    <Option Name="Include_test" Value="no" />
    <Option Name="SimpleInstall" Value="yes" />
    <Option Name="SimpleInstallDescription">Just for me, no test suite</Option>
</Options>
```

3.1.3 Installing Without Downloading

As some features of Python are not included in the initial installer download, selecting those features may require an internet connection. To avoid this need, all possible components may be downloaded on-demand to create a complete *layout* that will no longer require an internet connection regardless of the selected features. Note that this download may be bigger than required, but where a large number of installations are going to be performed it is very useful to have a locally cached copy.

Execute the following command from Command Prompt to download all possible required files. Remember to substitute `python-3.5.0.exe` for the actual name of your installer, and to create layouts in their own directories to avoid collisions between files with the same name.

```
python-3.5.0.exe /layout [optional target directory]
```

You may also specify the `/quiet` option to hide the progress display.

3.1.4 Other Platforms

With ongoing development of Python, some platforms that used to be supported earlier are no longer supported (due to the lack of users or developers). Check **PEP 11** for details on all unsupported platforms.

- Windows CE is still supported.
- The Cygwin installer offers to install the Python interpreter as well (cf. Cygwin package source, Maintainer releases)

See Python for Windows for detailed information about platforms with pre-compiled installers.

See also:

Python on XP "7 Minutes to "Hello World!"" by Richard Dooling, 2006

Installing on Windows in "Dive into Python: Python from novice to pro" by Mark Pilgrim, 2004, ISBN 1-59059-356-1

For Windows users in "Installing Python" in "A Byte of Python" by Swaroop C H, 2003

3.2 Alternative bundles

Besides the standard CPython distribution, there are modified packages including additional functionality. The following is a list of popular versions and their key features:

ActivePython Installer with multi-platform compatibility, documentation, PyWin32

Anaconda Popular scientific modules (such as numpy, scipy and pandas) and the `conda` package manager.

Canopy A "comprehensive Python analysis environment" with editors and other development tools.

WinPython Windows-specific distribution with prebuilt scientific packages and tools for building packages.

Note that these packages may not include the latest versions of Python or other libraries, and are not maintained or supported by the core Python team.

3.3 Configuring Python

To run Python conveniently from a command prompt, you might consider changing some default environment variables in Windows. While the installer provides an option to configure the PATH and PATHEXT variables for you, this is only reliable for a single, system-wide installation. If you regularly use multiple versions of Python, consider using the *Python Launcher for Windows*.

3.3.1 Excursus: Setting environment variables

Windows allows environment variables to be configured permanently at both the User level and the System level, or temporarily in a command prompt.

To temporarily set environment variables, open Command Prompt and use the **set** command:

```
C:\>set PATH=C:\Program Files\Python 3.5;%PATH%
C:\>set PYTHONPATH=%PYTHONPATH%;C:\My_python_lib
C:\>python
```

These changes will apply to any further commands executed in that console, and will be inherited by any applications started from the console.

Including the variable name within percent signs will expand to the existing value, allowing you to add your new value at either the start or the end. Modifying PATH by adding the directory containing **python.exe** to the start is a common way to ensure the correct version of Python is launched.

To permanently modify the default environment variables, click Start and search for 'edit environment variables', or open System properties, *Advanced system settings* and click the *Environment Variables* button. In this dialog, you can add or modify User and System variables. To change System variables, you need non-restricted access to your machine (i.e. Administrator rights).

Note: Windows will concatenate User variables *after* System variables, which may cause unexpected results when modifying PATH.

The PYTHONPATH variable is used by all versions of Python 2 and Python 3, so you should not permanently configure this variable unless it only includes code that is compatible with all of your installed Python versions.

See also:

http://support.microsoft.com/kb/100843 Environment variables in Windows NT

http://technet.microsoft.com/en-us/library/cc754250.aspx The SET command, for temporarily modifying environment variables

http://technet.microsoft.com/en-us/library/cc755104.aspx The SETX command, for permanently modifying environment variables

http://support.microsoft.com/kb/310519 How To Manage Environment Variables in Windows XP http://www.chem.gla.ac.uk/~louis/software/faq/q1.html Setting Environment variables, Louis J. Farrugia

3.3.2 Finding the Python executable

Changed in version 3.5.

Besides using the automatically created start menu entry for the Python interpreter, you might want to start Python in the command prompt. The installer for Python 3.5 and later has an option to set that up for you.

On the first page of the installer, an option labelled "Add Python 3.5 to PATH" can be selected to have the installer add the install location into the PATH. The location of the Scripts\ folder is also added. This allows you to type **python** to run the interpreter, and **pip** or . Thus, you can also execute your scripts with command line options, see *Command line* documentation.

If you don't enable this option at install time, you can always re-run the installer, select Modify, and enable it. Alternatively, you can manually modify the PATH using the directions in *Excursus: Setting environment variables*. You need to set your PATH environment variable to include the directory of your Python installation, delimited by a semicolon from other entries. An example variable could look like this (assuming the first two entries already existed):

```
C:\WINDOWS\system32;C:\WINDOWS;C:\Program Files\Python 3.5
```

3.4 Python Launcher for Windows

New in version 3.3.

The Python launcher for Windows is a utility which aids in locating and executing of different Python versions. It allows scripts (or the command-line) to indicate a preference for a specific Python version, and will locate and execute that version.

Unlike the PATH variable, the launcher will correctly select the most appropriate version of Python. It will prefer per-user installations over system-wide ones, and orders by language version rather than using the most recently installed version.

3.4.1 Getting started

From the command-line

System-wide installations of Python 3.3 and later will put the launcher on your PATH. The launcher is compatible with all available versions of Python, so it does not matter which version is installed. To check that the launcher is available, execute the following command in Command Prompt:

```
py
```

You should find that the latest version of Python 2.x you have installed is started - it can be exited as normal, and any additional command-line arguments specified will be sent directly to Python.

If you have multiple versions of Python 2.x installed (e.g., 2.6 and 2.7) you will have noticed that Python 2.7 was started - to launch Python 2.6, try the command:

```
py -2.6
```

If you have a Python 3.x installed, try the command:

```
py -3
```

You should find the latest version of Python 3.x starts.

If you see the following error, you do not have the launcher installed:

```
'py' is not recognized as an internal or external command,
operable program or batch file.
```

Per-user installations of Python do not add the launcher to PATH unless the option was selected on installation.

Virtual environments

New in version 3.5.

If the launcher is run with no explicit Python version specification, and a virtual environment (created with the standard library venv module or the external virtualenv tool) active, the launcher will run the virtual environment's interpreter rather than the global one. To run the global interpreter, either deactivate the virtual environment, or explicitly specify the global Python version.

From a script

Let's create a test Python script - create a file called hello.py with the following contents

```
#! python
import sys
sys.stdout.write("hello from Python %s\n" % (sys.version,))
```

From the directory in which hello.py lives, execute the command:

```
py hello.py
```

You should notice the version number of your latest Python 2.x installation is printed. Now try changing the first line to be:

```
#! python3
```

Re-executing the command should now print the latest Python 3.x information. As with the above command-line examples, you can specify a more explicit version qualifier. Assuming you have Python 2.6 installed, try changing the first line to #! python2.6 and you should find the 2.6 version information printed.

From file associations

The launcher should have been associated with Python files (i.e. .py, .pyw, .pyc files) when it was installed. This means that when you double-click on one of these files from Windows explorer the launcher will be used, and therefore you can use the same facilities described above to have the script specify the version which should be used.

The key benefit of this is that a single launcher can support multiple Python versions at the same time depending on the contents of the first line.

3.4.2 Shebang Lines

If the first line of a script file starts with #!, it is known as a "shebang" line. Linux and other Unix like operating systems have native support for such lines and are commonly used on such systems to indicate how a script should be executed. This launcher allows the same facilities to be using with Python scripts on Windows and the examples above demonstrate their use.

To allow shebang lines in Python scripts to be portable between Unix and Windows, this launcher supports a number of 'virtual' commands to specify which interpreter to use. The supported virtual commands are:

- `/usr/bin/env python`
- `/usr/bin/python`
- `/usr/local/bin/python`
- `python`

For example, if the first line of your script starts with

`#! /usr/bin/python`

The default Python will be located and used. As many Python scripts written to work on Unix will already have this line, you should find these scripts can be used by the launcher without modification. If you are writing a new script on Windows which you hope will be useful on Unix, you should use one of the shebang lines starting with `/usr`.

Any of the above virtual commands can be suffixed with an explicit version (either just the major version, or the major and minor version) - for example `/usr/bin/python2.7` - which will cause that specific version to be located and used.

The `/usr/bin/env` form of shebang line has one further special property. Before looking for installed Python interpreters, this form will search the executable `PATH` for a Python executable. This corresponds to the behaviour of the Unix `env` program, which performs a `PATH` search.

3.4.3 Arguments in shebang lines

The shebang lines can also specify additional options to be passed to the Python interpreter. For example, if you have a shebang line:

`#! /usr/bin/python -v`

Then Python will be started with the `-v` option

3.4.4 Customization

Customization via INI files

Two .ini files will be searched by the launcher - `py.ini` in the current user's "application data" directory (i.e. the directory returned by calling the Windows function SHGetFolderPath with CSIDL_LOCAL_APPDATA) and `py.ini` in the same directory as the launcher. The same .ini files are used for both the 'console' version of the launcher (i.e. py.exe) and for the 'windows' version (i.e. pyw.exe)

Customization specified in the "application directory" will have precedence over the one next to the executable, so a user, who may not have write access to the .ini file next to the launcher, can override commands in that global .ini file)

Customizing default Python versions

In some cases, a version qualifier can be included in a command to dictate which version of Python will be used by the command. A version qualifier starts with a major version number and can optionally be followed by a period ('.') and a minor version specifier. If the minor qualifier is specified, it may optionally be followed by "-32" to indicate the 32-bit implementation of that version be used.

For example, a shebang line of `#!python` has no version qualifier, while `#!python3` has a version qualifier which specifies only a major version.

If no version qualifiers are found in a command, the environment variable `PY_PYTHON` can be set to specify the default version qualifier - the default value is "2". Note this value could specify just a major version (e.g. "2") or a major.minor qualifier (e.g. "2.6"), or even major.minor-32.

If no minor version qualifiers are found, the environment variable PY_PYTHON{major} (where {major} is the current major version qualifier as determined above) can be set to specify the full version. If no such option is found, the launcher will enumerate the installed Python versions and use the latest minor release found for the major version, which is likely, although not guaranteed, to be the most recently installed version in that family.

On 64-bit Windows with both 32-bit and 64-bit implementations of the same (major.minor) Python version installed, the 64-bit version will always be preferred. This will be true for both 32-bit and 64-bit implementations of the launcher - a 32-bit launcher will prefer to execute a 64-bit Python installation of the specified version if available. This is so the behavior of the launcher can be predicted knowing only what versions are installed on the PC and without regard to the order in which they were installed (i.e., without knowing whether a 32 or 64-bit version of Python and corresponding launcher was installed last). As noted above, an optional "-32" suffix can be used on a version specifier to change this behaviour.

Examples:

- If no relevant options are set, the commands python and python2 will use the latest Python 2.x version installed and the command python3 will use the latest Python 3.x installed.

- The commands python3.1 and python2.7 will not consult any options at all as the versions are fully specified.

- If PY_PYTHON=3, the commands python and python3 will both use the latest installed Python 3 version.

- If PY_PYTHON=3.1-32, the command python will use the 32-bit implementation of 3.1 whereas the command python3 will use the latest installed Python (PY_PYTHON was not considered at all as a major version was specified.)

- If PY_PYTHON=3 and PY_PYTHON3=3.1, the commands python and python3 will both use specifically 3.1

In addition to environment variables, the same settings can be configured in the .INI file used by the launcher. The section in the INI file is called [defaults] and the key name will be the same as the environment variables without the leading PY_ prefix (and note that the key names in the INI file are case insensitive.) The contents of an environment variable will override things specified in the INI file.

For example:

- Setting PY_PYTHON=3.1 is equivalent to the INI file containing:

```
[defaults]
python=3.1
```

- Setting PY_PYTHON=3 and PY_PYTHON3=3.1 is equivalent to the INI file containing:

```
[defaults]
python=3
python3=3.1
```

3.4.5 Diagnostics

If an environment variable PYLAUNCH_DEBUG is set (to any value), the launcher will print diagnostic information to stderr (i.e. to the console). While this information manages to be simultaneously verbose *and* terse, it should allow you to see what versions of Python were located, why a particular version was chosen and the exact command-line used to execute the target Python.

3.5 Finding modules

Python usually stores its library (and thereby your site-packages folder) in the installation directory. So, if you had installed Python to `C:\Python\`, the default library would reside in `C:\Python\Lib\` and third-party modules should be stored in `C:\Python\Lib\site-packages\`.

This is how `sys.path` is populated on Windows:

- An empty entry is added at the start, which corresponds to the current directory.

- If the environment variable `PYTHONPATH` exists, as described in *Environment variables*, its entries are added next. Note that on Windows, paths in this variable must be separated by semicolons, to distinguish them from the colon used in drive identifiers (`C:\` etc.).

- Additional "application paths" can be added in the registry as subkeys of `\SOFTWARE\Python\PythonCore\version\PythonPath` under both the `HKEY_CURRENT_USER` and `HKEY_LOCAL_MACHINE` hives. Subkeys which have semicolon-delimited path strings as their default value will cause each path to be added to `sys.path`. (Note that all known installers only use HKLM, so HKCU is typically empty.)

- If the environment variable `PYTHONHOME` is set, it is assumed as "Python Home". Otherwise, the path of the main Python executable is used to locate a "landmark file" (`Lib\os.py`) to deduce the "Python Home". If a Python home is found, the relevant sub-directories added to `sys.path` (`Lib`, `plat-win`, etc) are based on that folder. Otherwise, the core Python path is constructed from the PythonPath stored in the registry.

- If the Python Home cannot be located, no `PYTHONPATH` is specified in the environment, and no registry entries can be found, a default path with relative entries is used (e.g. `.\Lib;.\plat-win`, etc).

If a `pyvenv.cfg` file is found alongside the main executable or in the directory one level above the executable, the following variations apply:

- If `home` is an absolute path and `PYTHONHOME` is not set, this path is used instead of the path to the main executable when deducing the home location.

- If `applocal` is set to true, the `home` property or the main executable is always used as the home path, and all environment variables or registry values affecting the path are ignored. The landmark file is not checked.

The end result of all this is:

- When running `python.exe`, or any other .exe in the main Python directory (either an installed version, or directly from the PCbuild directory), the core path is deduced, and the core paths in the registry are ignored. Other "application paths" in the registry are always read.

- When Python is hosted in another .exe (different directory, embedded via COM, etc), the "Python Home" will not be deduced, so the core path from the registry is used. Other "application paths" in the registry are always read.

- If Python can't find its home and there are no registry value (frozen .exe, some very strange installation setup) you get a path with some default, but relative, paths.

For those who want to bundle Python into their application or distribution, the following advice will prevent conflicts with other installations:

- Include a `pyvenv.cfg` file alongside your executable containing `applocal = true`. This will ensure that your own directory will be used to resolve paths even if you have included the standard library in a ZIP file. It will also ignore user site-packages and other paths listed in the registry.

- If you are loading `python3.dll` or `python35.dll` in your own executable, explicitly call `Py_SetPath()` or (at least) `Py_SetProgramName()` before `Py_Initialize()`.

- Clear and/or overwrite `PYTHONPATH` and set `PYTHONHOME` before launching `python.exe` from your application.

- If you cannot use the previous suggestions (for example, you are a distribution that allows people to run `python.exe` directly), ensure that the landmark file (`Lib\os.py`) exists in your install directory. (Note that it will not be detected inside a ZIP file.)

These will ensure that the files in a system-wide installation will not take precedence over the copy of the standard library bundled with your application. Otherwise, your users may experience problems using your application. Note that the first suggestion is the best, as the other may still be susceptible to non-standard paths in the registry and user site-packages.

3.6 Additional modules

Even though Python aims to be portable among all platforms, there are features that are unique to Windows. A couple of modules, both in the standard library and external, and snippets exist to use these features.

The Windows-specific standard modules are documented in *mswin-specific-services*.

3.6.1 PyWin32

The PyWin32 module by Mark Hammond is a collection of modules for advanced Windows-specific support. This includes utilities for:

- Component Object Model (**COM**)
- Win32 API calls
- Registry
- Event log
- Microsoft Foundation Classes (**MFC**) user interfaces

PythonWin is a sample MFC application shipped with PyWin32. It is an embeddable IDE with a built-in debugger.

See also:

Win32 How Do I...? by Tim Golden

Python and COM by David and Paul Boddie

3.6.2 cx_Freeze

cx_Freeze is a `distutils` extension (see *extending-distutils*) which wraps Python scripts into executable Windows programs (`*.exe` files). When you have done this, you can distribute your application without requiring your users to install Python.

3.6.3 WConio

Since Python's advanced terminal handling layer, `curses`, is restricted to Unix-like systems, there is a library exclusive to Windows as well: Windows Console I/O for Python.

WConio is a wrapper for Turbo-C's `CONIO.H`, used to create text user interfaces.

3.7 Compiling Python on Windows

If you want to compile CPython yourself, first thing you should do is get the source. You can download either the latest release's source or just grab a fresh checkout.

The source tree contains a build solution and project files for Microsoft Visual Studio 2015, which is the compiler used to build the official Python releases. These files are in the PCbuild directory.

Check PCbuild/readme.txt for general information on the build process.

For extension modules, consult *building-on-windows*.

See also:

Python + Windows + distutils + SWIG + gcc MinGW or "Creating Python extensions in C/C++ with SWIG and compiling them with MinGW gcc under Windows" or "Installing Python extension with distutils and without Microsoft Visual C++" by Sébastien Sauvage, 2003

MingW – Python extensions by Trent Apted et al, 2007

3.8 Embedded Distribution

New in version 3.5.

The embedded distribution is a ZIP file containing a minimal Python environment. It is intended for acting as part of another application, rather than being directly accessed by end-users.

When extracted, the embedded distribution is (almost) fully isolated from the user's system, including environment variables, system registry settings, and installed packages. The standard library is included as pre-compiled and optimized .pyc files in a ZIP, and python3.dll, python35.dll, python.exe and pythonw.exe are all provided. Tcl/tk (including all dependants, such as Idle), pip and the Python documentation are not included.

Note: The embedded distribution does not include the Microsoft C Runtime and it is the responsibility of the application installer to provide this. The runtime may have already been installed on a user's system previously or automatically via Windows Update, and can be detected by finding ucrtbase.dll in the system directory.

Third-party packages should be installed by the application installer alongside the embedded distribution. Using pip to manage dependencies as for a regular Python installation is not supported with this distribution, though with some care it may be possible to include and use pip for automatic updates. In general, third-party packages should be treated as part of the application ("vendoring") so that the developer can ensure compatibility with newer versions before providing updates to users.

The two recommended use cases for this distribution are described below.

3.8.1 Python Application

An application written in Python does not necessarily require users to be aware of that fact. The embedded distribution may be used in this case to include a private version of Python in an install package. Depending on how transparent it should be (or conversely, how professional it should appear), there are two options.

Using a specialized executable as a launcher requires some coding, but provides the most transparent experience for users. With a customized launcher, there are no obvious indications that the program is running on Python: icons can be customized, company and version information can be specified, and file associations behave properly. In most cases, a custom launcher should simply be able to call Py_Main with a hard-coded command line.

The simpler approach is to provide a batch file or generated shortcut that directly calls the `python.exe` or `pythonw.exe` with the required command-line arguments. In this case, the application will appear to be Python and not its actual name, and users may have trouble distinguishing it from other running Python processes or file associations.

With the latter approach, packages should be installed as directories alongside the Python executable to ensure they are available on the path. With the specialized launcher, packages can be located in other locations as there is an opportunity to specify the search path before launching the application.

3.8.2 Embedding Python

Applications written in native code often require some form of scripting language, and the embedded Python distribution can be used for this purpose. In general, the majority of the application is in native code, and some part will either invoke `python.exe` or directly use `python3.dll`. For either case, extracting the embedded distribution to a subdirectory of the application installation is sufficient to provide a loadable Python interpreter.

As with the application use, packages can be installed to any location as there is an opportunity to specify search paths before initializing the interpreter. Otherwise, there is no fundamental differences between using the embedded distribution and a regular installation.

3.9 Other resources

See also:

Python Programming On Win32 "Help for Windows Programmers" by Mark Hammond and Andy Robinson, O'Reilly Media, 2000, ISBN 1-56592-621-8

A Python for Windows Tutorial by Amanda Birmingham, 2004

PEP 397 - Python launcher for Windows The proposal for the launcher to be included in the Python distribution.

CHAPTER

FOUR

USING PYTHON ON A MACINTOSH

Author Bob Savage <bobsavage@mac.com>

Python on a Macintosh running Mac OS X is in principle very similar to Python on any other Unix platform, but there are a number of additional features such as the IDE and the Package Manager that are worth pointing out.

4.1 Getting and Installing MacPython

Mac OS X 10.8 comes with Python 2.7 pre-installed by Apple. If you wish, you are invited to install the most recent version of Python 3 from the Python website (https://www.python.org). A current "universal binary" build of Python, which runs natively on the Mac's new Intel and legacy PPC CPU's, is available there.

What you get after installing is a number of things:

- A `MacPython 3.4` folder in your `Applications` folder. In here you find IDLE, the development environment that is a standard part of official Python distributions; PythonLauncher, which handles double-clicking Python scripts from the Finder; and the "Build Applet" tool, which allows you to package Python scripts as standalone applications on your system.

- A framework `/Library/Frameworks/Python.framework`, which includes the Python executable and libraries. The installer adds this location to your shell path. To uninstall MacPython, you can simply remove these three things. A symlink to the Python executable is placed in /usr/local/bin/.

The Apple-provided build of Python is installed in `/System/Library/Frameworks/Python.framework` and `/usr/bin/python`, respectively. You should never modify or delete these, as they are Apple-controlled and are used by Apple- or third-party software. Remember that if you choose to install a newer Python version from python.org, you will have two different but functional Python installations on your computer, so it will be important that your paths and usages are consistent with what you want to do.

IDLE includes a help menu that allows you to access Python documentation. If you are completely new to Python you should start reading the tutorial introduction in that document.

If you are familiar with Python on other Unix platforms you should read the section on running Python scripts from the Unix shell.

4.1.1 How to run a Python script

Your best way to get started with Python on Mac OS X is through the IDLE integrated development environment, see section *The IDE* and use the Help menu when the IDE is running.

If you want to run Python scripts from the Terminal window command line or from the Finder you first need an editor to create your script. Mac OS X comes with a number of standard Unix command line editors, **vim** and **emacs** among them. If you want a more Mac-like editor, **BBEdit** or **TextWrangler** from Bare

Bones Software (see http://www.barebones.com/products/bbedit/index.html) are good choices, as is **TextMate** (see http://macromates.com/). Other editors include **Gvim** (http://macvim.org) and **Aquamacs** (http://aquamacs.org/).

To run your script from the Terminal window you must make sure that `/usr/local/bin` is in your shell search path.

To run your script from the Finder you have two options:

- Drag it to **PythonLauncher**

- Select **PythonLauncher** as the default application to open your script (or any .py script) through the finder Info window and double-click it. **PythonLauncher** has various preferences to control how your script is launched. Option-dragging allows you to change these for one invocation, or use its Preferences menu to change things globally.

4.1.2 Running scripts with a GUI

With older versions of Python, there is one Mac OS X quirk that you need to be aware of: programs that talk to the Aqua window manager (in other words, anything that has a GUI) need to be run in a special way. Use **pythonw** instead of **python** to start such scripts.

With Python 3.4, you can use either **python** or **pythonw**.

4.1.3 Configuration

Python on OS X honors all standard Unix environment variables such as `PYTHONPATH`, but setting these variables for programs started from the Finder is non-standard as the Finder does not read your `.profile` or `.cshrc` at startup. You need to create a file ~ `/.MacOSX/environment.plist`. See Apple's Technical Document QA1067 for details.

For more information on installation Python packages in MacPython, see section *Installing Additional Python Packages*.

4.2 The IDE

MacPython ships with the standard IDLE development environment. A good introduction to using IDLE can be found at https://hkn.eecs.berkeley.edu/~dyoo/python/idle_intro/index.html.

4.3 Installing Additional Python Packages

There are several methods to install additional Python packages:

- Packages can be installed via the standard Python distutils mode (`python setup.py install`).
- Many packages can also be installed via the **setuptools** extension or **pip** wrapper, see https://pip.pypa.io/.

4.4 GUI Programming on the Mac

There are several options for building GUI applications on the Mac with Python.

PyObjC is a Python binding to Apple's Objective-C/Cocoa framework, which is the foundation of most modern Mac development. Information on PyObjC is available from https://pythonhosted.org/pyobjc/.

The standard Python GUI toolkit is `tkinter`, based on the cross-platform Tk toolkit (http://www.tcl.tk). An Aqua-native version of Tk is bundled with OS X by Apple, and the latest version can be downloaded and installed from http://www.activestate.com; it can also be built from source.

wxPython is another popular cross-platform GUI toolkit that runs natively on Mac OS X. Packages and documentation are available from http://www.wxpython.org.

PyQt is another popular cross-platform GUI toolkit that runs natively on Mac OS X. More information can be found at http://www.riverbankcomputing.co.uk/software/pyqt/intro.

4.5 Distributing Python Applications on the Mac

The "Build Applet" tool that is placed in the MacPython 3.4 folder is fine for packaging small Python scripts on your own machine to run as a standard Mac application. This tool, however, is not robust enough to distribute Python applications to other users.

The standard tool for deploying standalone Python applications on the Mac is **py2app**. More information on installing and using py2app can be found at http://undefined.org/python/#py2app.

4.6 Other Resources

The MacPython mailing list is an excellent support resource for Python users and developers on the Mac:

https://www.python.org/community/sigs/current/pythonmac-sig/

Another useful resource is the MacPython wiki:

https://wiki.python.org/moin/MacPython

ADDITIONAL TOOLS AND SCRIPTS

5.1 pyvenv - Creating virtual environments

Creation of *virtual environments* is done by executing the `pyvenv` script:

```
pyvenv /path/to/new/virtual/environment
```

Running this command creates the target directory (creating any parent directories that don't exist already) and places a `pyvenv.cfg` file in it with a `home` key pointing to the Python installation the command was run from. It also creates a `bin` (or `Scripts` on Windows) subdirectory containing a copy of the `python` binary (or binaries, in the case of Windows). It also creates an (initially empty) `lib/pythonX.Y/site-packages` subdirectory (on Windows, this is `Lib\site-packages`).

See also:

Python Packaging User Guide: Creating and using virtual environments

On Windows, you may have to invoke the `pyvenv` script as follows, if you don't have the relevant PATH and PATHEXT settings:

```
c:\Temp>c:\Python35\python c:\Python35\Tools\Scripts\pyvenv.py myenv
```

or equivalently:

```
c:\Temp>c:\Python35\python -m venv myenv
```

The command, if run with `-h`, will show the available options:

```
usage: venv [-h] [--system-site-packages] [--symlinks] [--clear]
            [--upgrade] [--without-pip] ENV_DIR [ENV_DIR ...]

Creates virtual Python environments in one or more target directories.

positional arguments:
  ENV_DIR               A directory to create the environment in.

optional arguments:
  -h, --help            show this help message and exit
  --system-site-packages Give access to the global site-packages dir to the
                        virtual environment.
  --symlinks            Try to use symlinks rather than copies, when symlinks
                        are not the default for the platform.
  --copies              Try to use copies rather than symlinks, even when
                        symlinks are the default for the platform.
  --clear               Delete the environment directory if it already exists.
                        If not specified and the directory exists, an error is
```

```
                            raised.
--upgrade                   Upgrade the environment directory to use this version
                            of Python, assuming Python has been upgraded in-place.
--without-pip               Skips installing or upgrading pip in the virtual
                            environment (pip is bootstrapped by default)
```

Depending on how the `venv` functionality has been invoked, the usage message may vary slightly, e.g. referencing `pyvenv` rather than `venv`.

Changed in version 3.4: Installs pip by default, added the `--without-pip` and `--copies` options

Changed in version 3.4: In earlier versions, if the target directory already existed, an error was raised, unless the `--clear` or `--upgrade` option was provided. Now, if an existing directory is specified, its contents are removed and the directory is processed as if it had been newly created.

The created `pyvenv.cfg` file also includes the `include-system-site-packages` key, set to `true` if `venv` is run with the `--system-site-packages` option, `false` otherwise.

Unless the `--without-pip` option is given, `ensurepip` will be invoked to bootstrap `pip` into the virtual environment.

Multiple paths can be given to `pyvenv`, in which case an identical virtualenv will be created, according to the given options, at each provided path.

Once a venv has been created, it can be "activated" using a script in the venv's binary directory. The invocation of the script is platform-specific:

Platform	Shell	Command to activate virtual environment
Posix	bash/zsh	$ source <venv>/bin/activate
	fish	$. <venv>/bin/activate.fish
	csh/tcsh	$ source <venv>/bin/activate.csh
Windows	cmd.exe	C:> <venv>/Scripts/activate.bat
	PowerShell	PS C:> <venv>/Scripts/Activate.ps1

You don't specifically *need* to activate an environment; activation just prepends the venv's binary directory to your path, so that "python" invokes the venv's Python interpreter and you can run installed scripts without having to use their full path. However, all scripts installed in a venv should be runnable without activating it, and run with the venv's Python automatically.

You can deactivate a venv by typing "deactivate" in your shell. The exact mechanism is platform-specific: for example, the Bash activation script defines a "deactivate" function, whereas on Windows there are separate scripts called `deactivate.bat` and `Deactivate.ps1` which are installed when the venv is created.

New in version 3.4: `fish` and `csh` activation scripts.

GLOSSARY

>>> The default Python prompt of the interactive shell. Often seen for code examples which can be executed interactively in the interpreter.

. . . The default Python prompt of the interactive shell when entering code for an indented code block or within a pair of matching left and right delimiters (parentheses, square brackets or curly braces).

2to3 A tool that tries to convert Python 2.x code to Python 3.x code by handling most of the incompatibilities which can be detected by parsing the source and traversing the parse tree.

2to3 is available in the standard library as `lib2to3`; a standalone entry point is provided as `Tools/scripts/2to3`. See *2to3-reference*.

abstract base class Abstract base classes complement *duck-typing* by providing a way to define interfaces when other techniques like `hasattr()` would be clumsy or subtly wrong (for example with *magic methods*). ABCs introduce virtual subclasses, which are classes that don't inherit from a class but are still recognized by `isinstance()` and `issubclass()`; see the `abc` module documentation. Python comes with many built-in ABCs for data structures (in the `collections.abc` module), numbers (in the `numbers` module), streams (in the `io` module), import finders and loaders (in the `importlib.abc` module). You can create your own ABCs with the `abc` module.

argument A value passed to a *function* (or *method*) when calling the function. There are two kinds of argument:

- *keyword argument*: an argument preceded by an identifier (e.g. `name=`) in a function call or passed as a value in a dictionary preceded by `**`. For example, 3 and 5 are both keyword arguments in the following calls to `complex()`:

```
complex(real=3, imag=5)
complex(**{'real': 3, 'imag': 5})
```

- *positional argument*: an argument that is not a keyword argument. Positional arguments can appear at the beginning of an argument list and/or be passed as elements of an *iterable* preceded by `*`. For example, 3 and 5 are both positional arguments in the following calls:

```
complex(3, 5)
complex(*(3, 5))
```

Arguments are assigned to the named local variables in a function body. See the *calls* section for the rules governing this assignment. Syntactically, any expression can be used to represent an argument; the evaluated value is assigned to the local variable.

See also the *parameter* glossary entry, the FAQ question on *the difference between arguments and parameters*, and **PEP 362**.

asynchronous context manager An object which controls the environment seen in an `async with` statement by defining `__aenter__()` and `__aexit__()` methods. Introduced by **PEP 492**.

asynchronous iterable An object, that can be used in an `async for` statement. Must return an *awaitable* from its `__aiter__()` method, which should in turn be resolved in an *asynchronous iterator* object. Introduced by PEP 492.

asynchronous iterator An object that implements `__aiter__()` and `__anext__()` methods, that must return *awaitable* objects. `async for` resolves awaitable returned from asynchronous iterator's `__anext__()` method until it raises `StopAsyncIteration` exception. Introduced by PEP 492.

attribute A value associated with an object which is referenced by name using dotted expressions. For example, if an object *o* has an attribute *a* it would be referenced as *o.a*.

awaitable An object that can be used in an `await` expression. Can be a *coroutine* or an object with an `__await__()` method. See also PEP 492.

BDFL Benevolent Dictator For Life, a.k.a. Guido van Rossum, Python's creator.

binary file A *file object* able to read and write *bytes-like objects*.

> **See also:**
>
> A *text file* reads and writes `str` objects.

bytes-like object An object that supports the *bufferobjects* and can export a C-*contiguous* buffer. This includes all `bytes`, `bytearray`, and `array.array` objects, as well as many common `memoryview` objects. Bytes-like objects can be used for various operations that work with binary data; these include compression, saving to a binary file, and sending over a socket.

Some operations need the binary data to be mutable. The documentation often refers to these as "read-write bytes-like objects". Example mutable buffer objects include `bytearray` and a `memoryview` of a `bytearray`. Other operations require the binary data to be stored in immutable objects ("read-only bytes-like objects"); examples of these include `bytes` and a `memoryview` of a `bytes` object.

bytecode Python source code is compiled into bytecode, the internal representation of a Python program in the CPython interpreter. The bytecode is also cached in `.pyc` and `.pyo` files so that executing the same file is faster the second time (recompilation from source to bytecode can be avoided). This "intermediate language" is said to run on a *virtual machine* that executes the machine code corresponding to each bytecode. Do note that bytecodes are not expected to work between different Python virtual machines, nor to be stable between Python releases.

A list of bytecode instructions can be found in the documentation for *the dis module*.

class A template for creating user-defined objects. Class definitions normally contain method definitions which operate on instances of the class.

coercion The implicit conversion of an instance of one type to another during an operation which involves two arguments of the same type. For example, `int(3.15)` converts the floating point number to the integer 3, but in `3+4.5`, each argument is of a different type (one int, one float), and both must be converted to the same type before they can be added or it will raise a `TypeError`. Without coercion, all arguments of even compatible types would have to be normalized to the same value by the programmer, e.g., `float(3)+4.5` rather than just `3+4.5`.

complex number An extension of the familiar real number system in which all numbers are expressed as a sum of a real part and an imaginary part. Imaginary numbers are real multiples of the imaginary unit (the square root of -1), often written i in mathematics or j in engineering. Python has built-in support for complex numbers, which are written with this latter notation; the imaginary part is written with a j suffix, e.g., `3+1j`. To get access to complex equivalents of the `math` module, use `cmath`. Use of complex numbers is a fairly advanced mathematical feature. If you're not aware of a need for them, it's almost certain you can safely ignore them.

context manager An object which controls the environment seen in a `with` statement by defining `__enter__()` and `__exit__()` methods. See PEP 343.

contiguous A buffer is considered contiguous exactly if it is either *C-contiguous* or *Fortran contiguous*. Zero-dimensional buffers are C and Fortran contiguous. In one-dimensional arrays, the items must be layed out in memory next to each other, in order of increasing indexes starting from zero. In multidimensional C-contiguous arrays, the last index varies the fastest when visiting items in order of memory address. However, in Fortran contiguous arrays, the first index varies the fastest.

coroutine Coroutines is a more generalized form of subroutines. Subroutines are entered at one point and exited at another point. Coroutines can be entered, exited, and resumed at many different points. They can be implemented with the `async def` statement. See also **PEP 492**.

coroutine function A function which returns a *coroutine* object. A coroutine function may be defined with the `async def` statement, and may contain `await`, `async for`, and `async with` keywords. These were introduced by **PEP 492**.

CPython The canonical implementation of the Python programming language, as distributed on python.org. The term "CPython" is used when necessary to distinguish this implementation from others such as Jython or IronPython.

decorator A function returning another function, usually applied as a function transformation using the `@wrapper` syntax. Common examples for decorators are `classmethod()` and `staticmethod()`.

The decorator syntax is merely syntactic sugar, the following two function definitions are semantically equivalent:

```
def f(...):
    ...
f = staticmethod(f)

@staticmethod
def f(...):
    ...
```

The same concept exists for classes, but is less commonly used there. See the documentation for *function definitions* and *class definitions* for more about decorators.

descriptor Any object which defines the methods `__get__()`, `__set__()`, or `__delete__()`. When a class attribute is a descriptor, its special binding behavior is triggered upon attribute lookup. Normally, using *a.b* to get, set or delete an attribute looks up the object named *b* in the class dictionary for *a*, but if *b* is a descriptor, the respective descriptor method gets called. Understanding descriptors is a key to a deep understanding of Python because they are the basis for many features including functions, methods, properties, class methods, static methods, and reference to super classes.

For more information about descriptors' methods, see *descriptors*.

dictionary An associative array, where arbitrary keys are mapped to values. The keys can be any object with `__hash__()` and `__eq__()` methods. Called a hash in Perl.

docstring A string literal which appears as the first expression in a class, function or module. While ignored when the suite is executed, it is recognized by the compiler and put into the `__doc__` attribute of the enclosing class, function or module. Since it is available via introspection, it is the canonical place for documentation of the object.

duck-typing A programming style which does not look at an object's type to determine if it has the right interface; instead, the method or attribute is simply called or used ("If it looks like a duck and quacks like a duck, it must be a duck.") By emphasizing interfaces rather than specific types, well-designed code improves its flexibility by allowing polymorphic substitution. Duck-typing avoids tests using `type()` or `isinstance()`. (Note, however, that duck-typing can be complemented with *abstract base classes*.) Instead, it typically employs `hasattr()` tests or *EAFP* programming.

EAFP Easier to ask for forgiveness than permission. This common Python coding style assumes the existence of valid keys or attributes and catches exceptions if the assumption proves false. This clean and fast style is characterized by the presence of many `try` and `except` statements. The technique contrasts with the *LBYL* style common to many other languages such as C.

expression A piece of syntax which can be evaluated to some value. In other words, an expression is an accumulation of expression elements like literals, names, attribute access, operators or function calls which all return a value. In contrast to many other languages, not all language constructs are expressions. There are also *statement*s which cannot be used as expressions, such as `if`. Assignments are also statements, not expressions.

extension module A module written in C or C++, using Python's C API to interact with the core and with user code.

file object An object exposing a file-oriented API (with methods such as `read()` or `write()`) to an underlying resource. Depending on the way it was created, a file object can mediate access to a real on-disk file or to another type of storage or communication device (for example standard input/output, in-memory buffers, sockets, pipes, etc.). File objects are also called *file-like objects* or *streams*.

There are actually three categories of file objects: raw *binary files*, buffered *binary files* and *text files*. Their interfaces are defined in the `io` module. The canonical way to create a file object is by using the `open()` function.

file-like object A synonym for *file object*.

finder An object that tries to find the *loader* for a module. It must implement either a method named `find_loader()` or a method named `find_module()`. See **PEP 302** and **PEP 420** for details and `importlib.abc.Finder` for an *abstract base class*.

floor division Mathematical division that rounds down to nearest integer. The floor division operator is `//`. For example, the expression `11 // 4` evaluates to `2` in contrast to the `2.75` returned by float true division. Note that `(-11) // 4` is `-3` because that is `-2.75` rounded *downward*. See **PEP 238**.

function A series of statements which returns some value to a caller. It can also be passed zero or more *arguments* which may be used in the execution of the body. See also *parameter*, *method*, and the *function* section.

function annotation An arbitrary metadata value associated with a function parameter or return value. Its syntax is explained in section *function*. Annotations may be accessed via the `__annotations__` special attribute of a function object.

Python itself does not assign any particular meaning to function annotations. They are intended to be interpreted by third-party libraries or tools. See **PEP 3107**, which describes some of their potential uses.

__future__ A pseudo-module which programmers can use to enable new language features which are not compatible with the current interpreter.

By importing the `__future__` module and evaluating its variables, you can see when a new feature was first added to the language and when it becomes the default:

```
>>> import __future__
>>> __future__.division
_Feature((2, 2, 0, 'alpha', 2), (3, 0, 0, 'alpha', 0), 8192)
```

garbage collection The process of freeing memory when it is not used anymore. Python performs garbage collection via reference counting and a cyclic garbage collector that is able to detect and break reference cycles.

generator A function which returns a *generator iterator*. It looks like a normal function except that it contains `yield` expressions for producing a series of values usable in a for-loop or that can be retrieved one at a time with the `next()` function.

Usually refers to a generator function, but may refer to a *generator iterator* in some contexts. In cases where the intended meaning isn't clear, using the full terms avoids ambiguity.

generator iterator An object created by a *generator* function.

Each `yield` temporarily suspends processing, remembering the location execution state (including local variables and pending try-statements). When the *generator iterator* resumes, it picks-up where it left-off (in contrast to functions which start fresh on every invocation).

generator expression An expression that returns an iterator. It looks like a normal expression followed by a `for` expression defining a loop variable, range, and an optional `if` expression. The combined expression generates values for an enclosing function:

```
>>> sum(i*i for i in range(10))         # sum of squares 0, 1, 4, ... 81
285
```

generic function A function composed of multiple functions implementing the same operation for different types. Which implementation should be used during a call is determined by the dispatch algorithm.

See also the *single dispatch* glossary entry, the `functools.singledispatch()` decorator, and **PEP 443**.

GIL See *global interpreter lock*.

global interpreter lock The mechanism used by the *CPython* interpreter to assure that only one thread executes Python *bytecode* at a time. This simplifies the CPython implementation by making the object model (including critical built-in types such as `dict`) implicitly safe against concurrent access. Locking the entire interpreter makes it easier for the interpreter to be multi-threaded, at the expense of much of the parallelism afforded by multi-processor machines.

However, some extension modules, either standard or third-party, are designed so as to release the GIL when doing computationally-intensive tasks such as compression or hashing. Also, the GIL is always released when doing I/O.

Past efforts to create a "free-threaded" interpreter (one which locks shared data at a much finer granularity) have not been successful because performance suffered in the common single-processor case. It is believed that overcoming this performance issue would make the implementation much more complicated and therefore costlier to maintain.

hashable An object is *hashable* if it has a hash value which never changes during its lifetime (it needs a `__hash__()` method), and can be compared to other objects (it needs an `__eq__()` method). Hashable objects which compare equal must have the same hash value.

Hashability makes an object usable as a dictionary key and a set member, because these data structures use the hash value internally.

All of Python's immutable built-in objects are hashable, while no mutable containers (such as lists or dictionaries) are. Objects which are instances of user-defined classes are hashable by default; they all compare unequal (except with themselves), and their hash value is derived from their `id()`.

IDLE An Integrated Development Environment for Python. IDLE is a basic editor and interpreter environment which ships with the standard distribution of Python.

immutable An object with a fixed value. Immutable objects include numbers, strings and tuples. Such an object cannot be altered. A new object has to be created if a different value has to be stored. They play an important role in places where a constant hash value is needed, for example as a key in a dictionary.

import path A list of locations (or *path entries*) that are searched by the *path based finder* for modules to import. During import, this list of locations usually comes from `sys.path`, but for subpackages it may also come from the parent package's `__path__` attribute.

importing The process by which Python code in one module is made available to Python code in another module.

importer An object that both finds and loads a module; both a *finder* and *loader* object.

interactive Python has an interactive interpreter which means you can enter statements and expressions at the interpreter prompt, immediately execute them and see their results. Just launch `python` with no arguments (possibly by selecting it from your computer's main menu). It is a very powerful way to test out new ideas or inspect modules and packages (remember `help(x)`).

interpreted Python is an interpreted language, as opposed to a compiled one, though the distinction can be blurry because of the presence of the bytecode compiler. This means that source files can be run directly without explicitly creating an executable which is then run. Interpreted languages typically have a shorter development/debug cycle than compiled ones, though their programs generally also run more slowly. See also *interactive*.

interpreter shutdown When asked to shut down, the Python interpreter enters a special phase where it gradually releases all allocated resources, such as modules and various critical internal structures. It also makes several calls to the *garbage collector*. This can trigger the execution of code in user-defined destructors or weakref callbacks. Code executed during the shutdown phase can encounter various exceptions as the resources it relies on may not function anymore (common examples are library modules or the warnings machinery).

The main reason for interpreter shutdown is that the __main__ module or the script being run has finished executing.

iterable An object capable of returning its members one at a time. Examples of iterables include all sequence types (such as `list`, `str`, and `tuple`) and some non-sequence types like `dict`, *file objects*, and objects of any classes you define with an __iter__() or __getitem__() method. Iterables can be used in a `for` loop and in many other places where a sequence is needed (`zip()`, `map()`, ...). When an iterable object is passed as an argument to the built-in function `iter()`, it returns an iterator for the object. This iterator is good for one pass over the set of values. When using iterables, it is usually not necessary to call `iter()` or deal with iterator objects yourself. The `for` statement does that automatically for you, creating a temporary unnamed variable to hold the iterator for the duration of the loop. See also *iterator*, *sequence*, and *generator*.

iterator An object representing a stream of data. Repeated calls to the iterator's __next__() method (or passing it to the built-in function `next()`) return successive items in the stream. When no more data are available a `StopIteration` exception is raised instead. At this point, the iterator object is exhausted and any further calls to its __next__() method just raise `StopIteration` again. Iterators are required to have an __iter__() method that returns the iterator object itself so every iterator is also iterable and may be used in most places where other iterables are accepted. One notable exception is code which attempts multiple iteration passes. A container object (such as a `list`) produces a fresh new iterator each time you pass it to the `iter()` function or use it in a `for` loop. Attempting this with an iterator will just return the same exhausted iterator object used in the previous iteration pass, making it appear like an empty container.

More information can be found in *typeiter*.

key function A key function or collation function is a callable that returns a value used for sorting or ordering. For example, `locale.strxfrm()` is used to produce a sort key that is aware of locale specific sort conventions.

A number of tools in Python accept key functions to control how elements are ordered or grouped. They include `min()`, `max()`, `sorted()`, `list.sort()`, `heapq.merge()`, `heapq.nsmallest()`, `heapq.nlargest()`, and `itertools.groupby()`.

There are several ways to create a key function. For example. the `str.lower()` method can serve as a key function for case insensitive sorts. Alternatively, a key function can be built from a `lambda` expression such as `lambda r:  (r[0], r[2])`. Also, the `operator` module provides three key function constructors: `attrgetter()`, `itemgetter()`, and `methodcaller()`. See the *Sorting HOW TO* for examples of how to create and use key functions.

keyword argument See *argument*.

lambda An anonymous inline function consisting of a single *expression* which is evaluated when the function is called. The syntax to create a lambda function is `lambda [arguments]:  expression`

LBYL Look before you leap. This coding style explicitly tests for pre-conditions before making calls or lookups. This style contrasts with the *EAFP* approach and is characterized by the presence of many `if` statements.

In a multi-threaded environment, the LBYL approach can risk introducing a race condition between "the looking" and "the leaping". For example, the code, `if key in mapping: return mapping[key]` can fail if another thread removes *key* from *mapping* after the test, but before the lookup. This issue can be solved with locks or by using the EAFP approach.

list A built-in Python *sequence*. Despite its name it is more akin to an array in other languages than to a linked list since access to elements are O(1).

list comprehension A compact way to process all or part of the elements in a sequence and return a list with the results. `result = ['{:#04x}'.format(x) for x in range(256) if x % 2 == 0]` generates a list of strings containing even hex numbers (0x..) in the range from 0 to 255. The `if` clause is optional. If omitted, all elements in `range(256)` are processed.

loader An object that loads a module. It must define a method named `load_module()`. A loader is typically returned by a *finder*. See **PEP 302** for details and `importlib.abc.Loader` for an *abstract base class*.

mapping A container object that supports arbitrary key lookups and implements the methods specified in the `Mapping` or `MutableMapping` *abstract base classes*. Examples include `dict`, `collections.defaultdict`, `collections.OrderedDict` and `collections.Counter`.

meta path finder A finder returned by a search of `sys.meta_path`. Meta path finders are related to, but different from *path entry finders*.

metaclass The class of a class. Class definitions create a class name, a class dictionary, and a list of base classes. The metaclass is responsible for taking those three arguments and creating the class. Most object oriented programming languages provide a default implementation. What makes Python special is that it is possible to create custom metaclasses. Most users never need this tool, but when the need arises, metaclasses can provide powerful, elegant solutions. They have been used for logging attribute access, adding thread-safety, tracking object creation, implementing singletons, and many other tasks.

More information can be found in *metaclasses*.

method A function which is defined inside a class body. If called as an attribute of an instance of that class, the method will get the instance object as its first *argument* (which is usually called `self`). See *function* and *nested scope*.

method resolution order Method Resolution Order is the order in which base classes are searched for a member during lookup. See The Python 2.3 Method Resolution Order.

module An object that serves as an organizational unit of Python code. Modules have a namespace containing arbitrary Python objects. Modules are loaded into Python by the process of *importing*.

See also *package*.

module spec A namespace containing the import-related information used to load a module.

MRO See *method resolution order*.

mutable Mutable objects can change their value but keep their `id()`. See also *immutable*.

named tuple Any tuple-like class whose indexable elements are also accessible using named attributes (for example, `time.localtime()` returns a tuple-like object where the *year* is accessible either with an index such as `t[0]` or with a named attribute like `t.tm_year`).

A named tuple can be a built-in type such as `time.struct_time`, or it can be created with a regular class definition. A full featured named tuple can also be created with the factory function `collections.namedtuple()`. The latter approach automatically provides extra features such as a self-documenting representation like `Employee(name='jones', title='programmer')`.

namespace The place where a variable is stored. Namespaces are implemented as dictionaries. There are the local, global and built-in namespaces as well as nested namespaces in objects (in methods). Namespaces support modularity by preventing naming conflicts. For instance, the functions `builtins.open` and `os.open()`

are distinguished by their namespaces. Namespaces also aid readability and maintainability by making it clear which module implements a function. For instance, writing `random.seed()` or `itertools.islice()` makes it clear that those functions are implemented by the `random` and `itertools` modules, respectively.

namespace package A *PEP 420 package* which serves only as a container for subpackages. Namespace packages may have no physical representation, and specifically are not like a *regular package* because they have no `__init__.py` file.

See also *module*.

nested scope The ability to refer to a variable in an enclosing definition. For instance, a function defined inside another function can refer to variables in the outer function. Note that nested scopes by default work only for reference and not for assignment. Local variables both read and write in the innermost scope. Likewise, global variables read and write to the global namespace. The `nonlocal` allows writing to outer scopes.

new-style class Old name for the flavor of classes now used for all class objects. In earlier Python versions, only new-style classes could use Python's newer, versatile features like `__slots__`, descriptors, properties, `__getattribute__()`, class methods, and static methods.

object Any data with state (attributes or value) and defined behavior (methods). Also the ultimate base class of any *new-style class*.

package A Python *module* which can contain submodules or recursively, subpackages. Technically, a package is a Python module with an `__path__` attribute.

See also *regular package* and *namespace package*.

parameter A named entity in a *function* (or method) definition that specifies an *argument* (or in some cases, arguments) that the function can accept. There are five kinds of parameter:

- *positional-or-keyword*: specifies an argument that can be passed either *positionally* or as a *keyword argument*. This is the default kind of parameter, for example *foo* and *bar* in the following:

  ```
  def func(foo, bar=None): ...
  ```

- *positional-only*: specifies an argument that can be supplied only by position. Python has no syntax for defining positional-only parameters. However, some built-in functions have positional-only parameters (e.g. `abs()`).

- *keyword-only*: specifies an argument that can be supplied only by keyword. Keyword-only parameters can be defined by including a single var-positional parameter or bare `*` in the parameter list of the function definition before them, for example *kw_only1* and *kw_only2* in the following:

  ```
  def func(arg, *, kw_only1, kw_only2): ...
  ```

- *var-positional*: specifies that an arbitrary sequence of positional arguments can be provided (in addition to any positional arguments already accepted by other parameters). Such a parameter can be defined by prepending the parameter name with `*`, for example *args* in the following:

  ```
  def func(*args, **kwargs): ...
  ```

- *var-keyword*: specifies that arbitrarily many keyword arguments can be provided (in addition to any keyword arguments already accepted by other parameters). Such a parameter can be defined by prepending the parameter name with `**`, for example *kwargs* in the example above.

Parameters can specify both optional and required arguments, as well as default values for some optional arguments.

See also the *argument* glossary entry, the FAQ question on *the difference between arguments and parameters*, the `inspect.Parameter` class, the *function* section, and *PEP 362*.

path entry A single location on the *import path* which the *path based finder* consults to find modules for importing.

path entry finder A *finder* returned by a callable on `sys.path_hooks` (i.e. a *path entry hook*) which knows how to locate modules given a *path entry*.

path entry hook A callable on the `sys.path_hook` list which returns a *path entry finder* if it knows how to find modules on a specific *path entry*.

path based finder One of the default *meta path finders* which searches an *import path* for modules.

portion A set of files in a single directory (possibly stored in a zip file) that contribute to a namespace package, as defined in **PEP 420**.

positional argument See *argument*.

provisional API A provisional API is one which has been deliberately excluded from the standard library's backwards compatibility guarantees. While major changes to such interfaces are not expected, as long as they are marked provisional, backwards incompatible changes (up to and including removal of the interface) may occur if deemed necessary by core developers. Such changes will not be made gratuitously – they will occur only if serious fundamental flaws are uncovered that were missed prior to the inclusion of the API.

Even for provisional APIs, backwards incompatible changes are seen as a "solution of last resort" - every attempt will still be made to find a backwards compatible resolution to any identified problems.

This process allows the standard library to continue to evolve over time, without locking in problematic design errors for extended periods of time. See **PEP 411** for more details.

provisional package See *provisional API*.

Python 3000 Nickname for the Python 3.x release line (coined long ago when the release of version 3 was something in the distant future.) This is also abbreviated "Py3k".

Pythonic An idea or piece of code which closely follows the most common idioms of the Python language, rather than implementing code using concepts common to other languages. For example, a common idiom in Python is to loop over all elements of an iterable using a `for` statement. Many other languages don't have this type of construct, so people unfamiliar with Python sometimes use a numerical counter instead:

```
for i in range(len(food)):
    print(food[i])
```

As opposed to the cleaner, Pythonic method:

```
for piece in food:
    print(piece)
```

qualified name A dotted name showing the "path" from a module's global scope to a class, function or method defined in that module, as defined in **PEP 3155**. For top-level functions and classes, the qualified name is the same as the object's name:

```
>>> class C:
...     class D:
...         def meth(self):
...             pass
...
>>> C.__qualname__
'C'
>>> C.D.__qualname__
'C.D'
>>> C.D.meth.__qualname__
'C.D.meth'
```

When used to refer to modules, the *fully qualified name* means the entire dotted path to the module, including any parent packages, e.g. `email.mime.text`:

```
>>> import email.mime.text
>>> email.mime.text.__name__
'email.mime.text'
```

reference count The number of references to an object. When the reference count of an object drops to zero, it is deallocated. Reference counting is generally not visible to Python code, but it is a key element of the *CPython* implementation. The `sys` module defines a `getrefcount()` function that programmers can call to return the reference count for a particular object.

regular package A traditional *package*, such as a directory containing an `__init__.py` file.

See also *namespace package*.

__slots__ A declaration inside a class that saves memory by pre-declaring space for instance attributes and eliminating instance dictionaries. Though popular, the technique is somewhat tricky to get right and is best reserved for rare cases where there are large numbers of instances in a memory-critical application.

sequence An *iterable* which supports efficient element access using integer indices via the `__getitem__()` special method and defines a `__len__()` method that returns the length of the sequence. Some built-in sequence types are `list`, `str`, `tuple`, and `bytes`. Note that `dict` also supports `__getitem__()` and `__len__()`, but is considered a mapping rather than a sequence because the lookups use arbitrary *immutable* keys rather than integers.

The `collections.abc.Sequence` abstract base class defines a much richer interface that goes beyond just `__getitem__()` and `__len__()`, adding `count()`, `index()`, `__contains__()`, and `__reversed__()`. Types that implement this expanded interface can be registered explicitly using `register()`.

single dispatch A form of *generic function* dispatch where the implementation is chosen based on the type of a single argument.

slice An object usually containing a portion of a *sequence*. A slice is created using the subscript notation, `[]` with colons between numbers when several are given, such as in `variable_name[1:3:5]`. The bracket (subscript) notation uses `slice` objects internally.

special method A method that is called implicitly by Python to execute a certain operation on a type, such as addition. Such methods have names starting and ending with double underscores. Special methods are documented in *specialnames*.

statement A statement is part of a suite (a "block" of code). A statement is either an *expression* or one of several constructs with a keyword, such as `if`, `while` or `for`.

struct sequence A tuple with named elements. Struct sequences expose an interface similar to *named tuple* in that elements can either be accessed either by index or as an attribute. However, they do not have any of the named tuple methods like `_make()` or `_asdict()`. Examples of struct sequences include `sys.float_info` and the return value of `os.stat()`.

text encoding A codec which encodes Unicode strings to bytes.

text file A *file object* able to read and write `str` objects. Often, a text file actually accesses a byte-oriented datastream and handles the *text encoding* automatically.

See also:

A *binary file* reads and write `bytes` objects.

triple-quoted string A string which is bound by three instances of either a quotation mark (") or an apostrophe ('). While they don't provide any functionality not available with single-quoted strings, they are useful for a number of reasons. They allow you to include unescaped single and double quotes within a string and they can span multiple lines without the use of the continuation character, making them especially useful when writing docstrings.

type The type of a Python object determines what kind of object it is; every object has a type. An object's type is accessible as its `__class__` attribute or can be retrieved with `type(obj)`.

universal newlines A manner of interpreting text streams in which all of the following are recognized as ending a line: the Unix end-of-line convention `'\n'`, the Windows convention `'\r\n'`, and the old Macintosh convention `'\r'`. See PEP 278 and PEP 3116, as well as `bytes.splitlines()` for an additional use.

view The objects returned from `dict.keys()`, `dict.values()`, and `dict.items()` are called dictionary views. They are lazy sequences that will see changes in the underlying dictionary. To force the dictionary view to become a full list use `list(dictview)`. See *dict-views*.

virtual environment A cooperatively isolated runtime environment that allows Python users and applications to install and upgrade Python distribution packages without interfering with the behaviour of other Python applications running on the same system.

See also *pyvenv - Creating virtual environments*

virtual machine A computer defined entirely in software. Python's virtual machine executes the *bytecode* emitted by the bytecode compiler.

Zen of Python Listing of Python design principles and philosophies that are helpful in understanding and using the language. The listing can be found by typing "`import this`" at the interactive prompt.

ABOUT THESE DOCUMENTS

These documents are generated from reStructuredText sources by Sphinx, a document processor specifically written for the Python documentation.

Development of the documentation and its toolchain is an entirely volunteer effort, just like Python itself. If you want to contribute, please take a look at the *reporting-bugs* page for information on how to do so. New volunteers are always welcome!

Many thanks go to:

- Fred L. Drake, Jr., the creator of the original Python documentation toolset and writer of much of the content;
- the Docutils project for creating reStructuredText and the Docutils suite;
- Fredrik Lundh for his Alternative Python Reference project from which Sphinx got many good ideas.

B.1 Contributors to the Python Documentation

Many people have contributed to the Python language, the Python standard library, and the Python documentation. See Misc/ACKS in the Python source distribution for a partial list of contributors.

It is only with the input and contributions of the Python community that Python has such wonderful documentation – Thank You!

HISTORY AND LICENSE

C.1 History of the software

Python was created in the early 1990s by Guido van Rossum at Stichting Mathematisch Centrum (CWI, see http://www.cwi.nl/) in the Netherlands as a successor of a language called ABC. Guido remains Python's principal author, although it includes many contributions from others.

In 1995, Guido continued his work on Python at the Corporation for National Research Initiatives (CNRI, see http://www.cnri.reston.va.us/) in Reston, Virginia where he released several versions of the software.

In May 2000, Guido and the Python core development team moved to BeOpen.com to form the BeOpen Python-Labs team. In October of the same year, the PythonLabs team moved to Digital Creations (now Zope Corporation; see http://www.zope.com/). In 2001, the Python Software Foundation (PSF, see https://www.python.org/psf/) was formed, a non-profit organization created specifically to own Python-related Intellectual Property. Zope Corporation is a sponsoring member of the PSF.

All Python releases are Open Source (see http://opensource.org/ for the Open Source Definition). Historically, most, but not all, Python releases have also been GPL-compatible; the table below summarizes the various releases.

Release	Derived from	Year	Owner	GPL compatible?
0.9.0 thru 1.2	n/a	1991-1995	CWI	yes
1.3 thru 1.5.2	1.2	1995-1999	CNRI	yes
1.6	1.5.2	2000	CNRI	no
2.0	1.6	2000	BeOpen.com	no
1.6.1	1.6	2001	CNRI	no
2.1	2.0+1.6.1	2001	PSF	no
2.0.1	2.0+1.6.1	2001	PSF	yes
2.1.1	2.1+2.0.1	2001	PSF	yes
2.1.2	2.1.1	2002	PSF	yes
2.1.3	2.1.2	2002	PSF	yes
2.2 and above	2.1.1	2001-now	PSF	yes

Note: GPL-compatible doesn't mean that we're distributing Python under the GPL. All Python licenses, unlike the GPL, let you distribute a modified version without making your changes open source. The GPL-compatible licenses make it possible to combine Python with other software that is released under the GPL; the others don't.

Thanks to the many outside volunteers who have worked under Guido's direction to make these releases possible.

C.2 Terms and conditions for accessing or otherwise using Python

PSF LICENSE AGREEMENT FOR PYTHON 3.5.0rc1

1. This LICENSE AGREEMENT is between the Python Software Foundation ("PSF"), and the Individual or Organization ("Licensee") accessing and otherwise using Python 3.5.0rc1 software in source or binary form and its associated documentation.

2. Subject to the terms and conditions of this License Agreement, PSF hereby grants Licensee a nonexclusive, royalty-free, world-wide license to reproduce, analyze, test, perform and/or display publicly, prepare derivative works, distribute, and otherwise use Python 3.5.0rc1 alone or in any derivative version, provided, however, that PSF's License Agreement and PSF's notice of copyright, i.e., "Copyright © 2001-2015 Python Software Foundation; All Rights Reserved" are retained in Python 3.5.0rc1 alone or in any derivative version prepared by Licensee.

3. In the event Licensee prepares a derivative work that is based on or incorporates Python 3.5.0rc1 or any part thereof, and wants to make the derivative work available to others as provided herein, then Licensee hereby agrees to include in any such work a brief summary of the changes made to Python 3.5.0rc1.

4. PSF is making Python 3.5.0rc1 available to Licensee on an "AS IS" basis. PSF MAKES NO REPRESENTATIONS OR WARRANTIES, EXPRESS OR IMPLIED. BY WAY OF EXAMPLE, BUT NOT LIMITATION, PSF MAKES NO AND DISCLAIMS ANY REPRESENTATION OR WARRANTY OF MERCHANTABILITY OR FITNESS FOR ANY PARTICULAR PURPOSE OR THAT THE USE OF PYTHON 3.5.0rc1 WILL NOT INFRINGE ANY THIRD PARTY RIGHTS.

5. PSF SHALL NOT BE LIABLE TO LICENSEE OR ANY OTHER USERS OF PYTHON 3.5.0rc1 FOR ANY INCIDENTAL, SPECIAL, OR CONSEQUENTIAL DAMAGES OR LOSS AS A RESULT OF MODIFYING, DISTRIBUTING, OR OTHERWISE USING PYTHON 3.5.0rc1, OR ANY DERIVATIVE THEREOF, EVEN IF ADVISED OF THE POSSIBILITY THEREOF.

6. This License Agreement will automatically terminate upon a material breach of its terms and conditions.

7. Nothing in this License Agreement shall be deemed to create any relationship of agency, partnership, or joint venture between PSF and Licensee. This License Agreement does not grant permission to use PSF trademarks or trade name in a trademark sense to endorse or promote products or services of Licensee, or any third party.

8. By copying, installing or otherwise using Python 3.5.0rc1, Licensee agrees to be bound by the terms and conditions of this License Agreement.

BEOPEN.COM LICENSE AGREEMENT FOR PYTHON 2.0

BEOPEN PYTHON OPEN SOURCE LICENSE AGREEMENT VERSION 1

1. This LICENSE AGREEMENT is between BeOpen.com ("BeOpen"), having an office at 160 Saratoga Avenue, Santa Clara, CA 95051, and the Individual or Organization ("Licensee") accessing and otherwise using this software in source or binary form and its associated documentation ("the Software").

2. Subject to the terms and conditions of this BeOpen Python License Agreement, BeOpen hereby grants Licensee a non-exclusive, royalty-free, world-wide license to reproduce, analyze, test, perform and/or display publicly, prepare derivative works, distribute, and otherwise use the Software alone or in any derivative version, provided, however, that the BeOpen Python License is retained in the Software, alone or in any derivative version prepared by Licensee.

3. BeOpen is making the Software available to Licensee on an "AS IS" basis. BEOPEN MAKES NO REPRESENTATIONS OR WARRANTIES, EXPRESS OR IMPLIED. BY WAY OF EXAMPLE, BUT NOT LIMITATION, BEOPEN MAKES NO AND DISCLAIMS ANY REPRESENTATION OR WARRANTY OF MERCHANTABILITY OR FITNESS FOR ANY PARTICULAR PURPOSE OR THAT THE USE OF THE SOFTWARE WILL NOT INFRINGE ANY THIRD PARTY RIGHTS.

4. BEOPEN SHALL NOT BE LIABLE TO LICENSEE OR ANY OTHER USERS OF THE SOFTWARE FOR ANY INCIDENTAL, SPECIAL, OR CONSEQUENTIAL DAMAGES OR LOSS AS A RESULT OF USING, MODIFYING OR DISTRIBUTING THE SOFTWARE, OR ANY DERIVATIVE THEREOF, EVEN IF ADVISED OF THE POSSIBILITY THEREOF.

5. This License Agreement will automatically terminate upon a material breach of its terms and conditions.

6. This License Agreement shall be governed by and interpreted in all respects by the law of the State of California, excluding conflict of law provisions. Nothing in this License Agreement shall be deemed to create any relationship of agency, partnership, or joint venture between BeOpen and Licensee. This License Agreement does not grant permission to use BeOpen trademarks or trade names in a trademark sense to endorse or promote products or services of Licensee, or any third party. As an exception, the "BeOpen Python" logos available at http://www.pythonlabs.com/logos.html may be used according to the permissions granted on that web page.

7. By copying, installing or otherwise using the software, Licensee agrees to be bound by the terms and conditions of this License Agreement.

CNRI LICENSE AGREEMENT FOR PYTHON 1.6.1

1. This LICENSE AGREEMENT is between the Corporation for National Research Initiatives, having an office at 1895 Preston White Drive, Reston, VA 20191 ("CNRI"), and the Individual or Organization ("Licensee") accessing and otherwise using Python 1.6.1 software in source or binary form and its associated documentation.

2. Subject to the terms and conditions of this License Agreement, CNRI hereby grants Licensee a nonexclusive, royalty-free, world-wide license to reproduce, analyze, test, perform and/or display publicly, prepare derivative works, distribute, and otherwise use Python 1.6.1 alone or in any derivative version, provided, however, that CNRI's License Agreement and CNRI's notice of copyright, i.e., "Copyright © 1995-2001 Corporation for National Research Initiatives; All Rights Reserved" are retained in Python 1.6.1 alone or in any derivative version prepared by Licensee. Alternately, in lieu of CNRI's License Agreement, Licensee may substitute the following text (omitting the quotes): "Python 1.6.1 is made available subject to the terms and conditions in CNRI's License Agreement. This Agreement together with Python 1.6.1 may be located on the Internet using the following unique, persistent identifier (known as a handle): 1895.22/1013. This Agreement may also be obtained from a proxy server on the Internet using the following URL: http://hdl.handle.net/1895.22/1013."

3. In the event Licensee prepares a derivative work that is based on or incorporates Python 1.6.1 or any part thereof, and wants to make the derivative work available to others as provided herein, then Licensee hereby agrees to include in any such work a brief summary of the changes made to Python 1.6.1.

4. CNRI is making Python 1.6.1 available to Licensee on an "AS IS" basis. CNRI MAKES NO REPRESENTATIONS OR WARRANTIES, EXPRESS OR IMPLIED. BY WAY OF EXAMPLE, BUT NOT LIMITATION, CNRI MAKES NO AND DISCLAIMS ANY REPRESENTATION OR WARRANTY OF MERCHANTABILITY OR FITNESS FOR ANY PARTICULAR PURPOSE OR THAT THE USE OF PYTHON 1.6.1 WILL NOT INFRINGE ANY THIRD PARTY RIGHTS.

5. CNRI SHALL NOT BE LIABLE TO LICENSEE OR ANY OTHER USERS OF PYTHON 1.6.1 FOR ANY INCIDENTAL, SPECIAL, OR CONSEQUENTIAL DAMAGES OR LOSS AS A RESULT OF MODIFYING, DISTRIBUTING, OR OTHERWISE USING PYTHON 1.6.1, OR ANY DERIVATIVE THEREOF, EVEN IF ADVISED OF THE POSSIBILITY THEREOF.

6. This License Agreement will automatically terminate upon a material breach of its terms and conditions.

7. This License Agreement shall be governed by the federal intellectual property law of the United States, including without limitation the federal copyright law, and, to the extent such U.S. federal law does not apply, by the law of the Commonwealth of Virginia, excluding Virginia's conflict of law provisions. Notwithstanding the foregoing, with regard to derivative works based on Python 1.6.1 that incorporate non-separable material that was previously distributed under the GNU General Public License (GPL), the law of the Commonwealth of Virginia shall govern this License Agreement only as to issues arising under or with respect to Paragraphs 4, 5, and 7 of this License Agreement. Nothing in this License Agreement shall be deemed to create any relationship of agency, partnership, or joint venture between CNRI and Licensee. This License Agreement does not grant permission to use CNRI trademarks or trade name in a trademark sense to endorse or promote products or services of Licensee, or any third party.

8. By clicking on the "ACCEPT" button where indicated, or by copying, installing or otherwise using Python 1.6.1, Licensee agrees to be bound by the terms and conditions of this License Agreement.

ACCEPT

CWI LICENSE AGREEMENT FOR PYTHON 0.9.0 THROUGH 1.2

Copyright © 1991 - 1995, Stichting Mathematisch Centrum Amsterdam, The Netherlands. All rights reserved.

Permission to use, copy, modify, and distribute this software and its documentation for any purpose and without fee is hereby granted, provided that the above copyright notice appear in all copies and that both that copyright notice and this permission notice appear in supporting documentation, and that the name of Stichting Mathematisch Centrum or CWI not be used in advertising or publicity pertaining to distribution of the software without specific, written prior permission.

STICHTING MATHEMATISCH CENTRUM DISCLAIMS ALL WARRANTIES WITH REGARD TO THIS SOFT-WARE, INCLUDING ALL IMPLIED WARRANTIES OF MERCHANTABILITY AND FITNESS, IN NO EVENT SHALL STICHTING MATHEMATISCH CENTRUM BE LIABLE FOR ANY SPECIAL, INDIRECT OR CON-SEQUENTIAL DAMAGES OR ANY DAMAGES WHATSOEVER RESULTING FROM LOSS OF USE, DATA OR PROFITS, WHETHER IN AN ACTION OF CONTRACT, NEGLIGENCE OR OTHER TORTIOUS ACTION, ARISING OUT OF OR IN CONNECTION WITH THE USE OR PERFORMANCE OF THIS SOFTWARE.

C.3 Licenses and Acknowledgements for Incorporated Software

This section is an incomplete, but growing list of licenses and acknowledgements for third-party software incorporated in the Python distribution.

C.3.1 Mersenne Twister

The `_random` module includes code based on a download from http://www.math.sci.hiroshima-u.ac.jp/~m-mat/MT/MT2002/emt19937ar.html. The following are the verbatim comments from the original code:

```
A C-program for MT19937, with initialization improved 2002/1/26.
Coded by Takuji Nishimura and Makoto Matsumoto.

Before using, initialize the state by using init_genrand(seed)
or init_by_array(init_key, key_length).

Copyright (C) 1997 - 2002, Makoto Matsumoto and Takuji Nishimura,
All rights reserved.

Redistribution and use in source and binary forms, with or without
modification, are permitted provided that the following conditions
are met:

  1. Redistributions of source code must retain the above copyright
     notice, this list of conditions and the following disclaimer.

  2. Redistributions in binary form must reproduce the above copyright
     notice, this list of conditions and the following disclaimer in the
     documentation and/or other materials provided with the distribution.

  3. The names of its contributors may not be used to endorse or promote
     products derived from this software without specific prior written
     permission.

THIS SOFTWARE IS PROVIDED BY THE COPYRIGHT HOLDERS AND CONTRIBUTORS
"AS IS" AND ANY EXPRESS OR IMPLIED WARRANTIES, INCLUDING, BUT NOT
```

```
LIMITED TO, THE IMPLIED WARRANTIES OF MERCHANTABILITY AND FITNESS FOR
A PARTICULAR PURPOSE ARE DISCLAIMED.  IN NO EVENT SHALL THE COPYRIGHT OWNER OR
CONTRIBUTORS BE LIABLE FOR ANY DIRECT, INDIRECT, INCIDENTAL, SPECIAL,
EXEMPLARY, OR CONSEQUENTIAL DAMAGES (INCLUDING, BUT NOT LIMITED TO,
PROCUREMENT OF SUBSTITUTE GOODS OR SERVICES; LOSS OF USE, DATA, OR
PROFITS; OR BUSINESS INTERRUPTION) HOWEVER CAUSED AND ON ANY THEORY OF
LIABILITY, WHETHER IN CONTRACT, STRICT LIABILITY, OR TORT (INCLUDING
NEGLIGENCE OR OTHERWISE) ARISING IN ANY WAY OUT OF THE USE OF THIS
SOFTWARE, EVEN IF ADVISED OF THE POSSIBILITY OF SUCH DAMAGE.


Any feedback is very welcome.
http://www.math.sci.hiroshima-u.ac.jp/~m-mat/MT/emt.html
email: m-mat @ math.sci.hiroshima-u.ac.jp (remove space)
```

C.3.2 Sockets

The `socket` module uses the functions, `getaddrinfo()`, and `getnameinfo()`, which are coded in separate source files from the WIDE Project, http://www.wide.ad.jp/.

```
Copyright (C) 1995, 1996, 1997, and 1998 WIDE Project.
All rights reserved.

Redistribution and use in source and binary forms, with or without
modification, are permitted provided that the following conditions
are met:
1. Redistributions of source code must retain the above copyright
   notice, this list of conditions and the following disclaimer.
2. Redistributions in binary form must reproduce the above copyright
   notice, this list of conditions and the following disclaimer in the
   documentation and/or other materials provided with the distribution.
3. Neither the name of the project nor the names of its contributors
   may be used to endorse or promote products derived from this software
   without specific prior written permission.

THIS SOFTWARE IS PROVIDED BY THE PROJECT AND CONTRIBUTORS ``AS IS'' AND
GAI_ANY EXPRESS OR IMPLIED WARRANTIES, INCLUDING, BUT NOT LIMITED TO, THE
IMPLIED WARRANTIES OF MERCHANTABILITY AND FITNESS FOR A PARTICULAR PURPOSE
ARE DISCLAIMED.  IN NO EVENT SHALL THE PROJECT OR CONTRIBUTORS BE LIABLE
FOR GAI_ANY DIRECT, INDIRECT, INCIDENTAL, SPECIAL, EXEMPLARY, OR CONSEQUENTIAL
DAMAGES (INCLUDING, BUT NOT LIMITED TO, PROCUREMENT OF SUBSTITUTE GOODS
OR SERVICES; LOSS OF USE, DATA, OR PROFITS; OR BUSINESS INTERRUPTION)
HOWEVER CAUSED AND ON GAI_ANY THEORY OF LIABILITY, WHETHER IN CONTRACT, STRICT
LIABILITY, OR TORT (INCLUDING NEGLIGENCE OR OTHERWISE) ARISING IN GAI_ANY WAY
OUT OF THE USE OF THIS SOFTWARE, EVEN IF ADVISED OF THE POSSIBILITY OF
SUCH DAMAGE.
```

C.3.3 Floating point exception control

The source for the `fpectl` module includes the following notice:

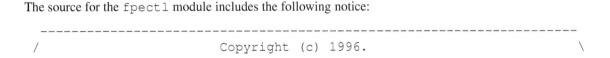

```
        ---------------------------------------------------------------------
    /                        Copyright (c) 1996.                          \
```

```
CONSEQUENTIAL DAMAGES OR ANY DAMAGES WHATSOEVER RESULTING FROM LOSS
OF USE, DATA OR PROFITS, WHETHER IN AN ACTION OF CONTRACT,
NEGLIGENCE OR OTHER TORTIOUS ACTION, ARISING OUT OF OR IN
CONNECTION WITH THE USE OR PERFORMANCE OF THIS SOFTWARE.
```

C.3.5 Cookie management

The `http.cookies` module contains the following notice:

```
Copyright 2000 by Timothy O'Malley <timo@alum.mit.edu>

              All Rights Reserved

Permission to use, copy, modify, and distribute this software
and its documentation for any purpose and without fee is hereby
granted, provided that the above copyright notice appear in all
copies and that both that copyright notice and this permission
notice appear in supporting documentation, and that the name of
Timothy O'Malley  not be used in advertising or publicity
pertaining to distribution of the software without specific, written
prior permission.

Timothy O'Malley DISCLAIMS ALL WARRANTIES WITH REGARD TO THIS
SOFTWARE, INCLUDING ALL IMPLIED WARRANTIES OF MERCHANTABILITY
AND FITNESS, IN NO EVENT SHALL Timothy O'Malley BE LIABLE FOR
ANY SPECIAL, INDIRECT OR CONSEQUENTIAL DAMAGES OR ANY DAMAGES
WHATSOEVER RESULTING FROM LOSS OF USE, DATA OR PROFITS,
WHETHER IN AN ACTION OF CONTRACT, NEGLIGENCE OR OTHER TORTIOUS
ACTION, ARISING OUT OF OR IN CONNECTION WITH THE USE OR
PERFORMANCE OF THIS SOFTWARE.
```

C.3.6 Execution tracing

The `trace` module contains the following notice:

```
portions copyright 2001, Autonomous Zones Industries, Inc., all rights...
err...  reserved and offered to the public under the terms of the
Python 2.2 license.
Author: Zooko O'Whielacronx
http://zooko.com/
mailto:zooko@zooko.com

Copyright 2000, Mojam Media, Inc., all rights reserved.
Author: Skip Montanaro

Copyright 1999, Bioreason, Inc., all rights reserved.
Author: Andrew Dalke

Copyright 1995-1997, Automatrix, Inc., all rights reserved.
Author: Skip Montanaro

Copyright 1991-1995, Stichting Mathematisch Centrum, all rights reserved.
```

```
Permission to use, copy, modify, and distribute this Python software and
its associated documentation for any purpose without fee is hereby
granted, provided that the above copyright notice appears in all copies,
and that both that copyright notice and this permission notice appear in
supporting documentation, and that the name of neither Automatrix,
Bioreason or Mojam Media be used in advertising or publicity pertaining to
distribution of the software without specific, written prior permission.
```

C.3.7 UUencode and UUdecode functions

The uu module contains the following notice:

```
Copyright 1994 by Lance Ellinghouse
Cathedral City, California Republic, United States of America.
                    All Rights Reserved
Permission to use, copy, modify, and distribute this software and its
documentation for any purpose and without fee is hereby granted,
provided that the above copyright notice appear in all copies and that
both that copyright notice and this permission notice appear in
supporting documentation, and that the name of Lance Ellinghouse
not be used in advertising or publicity pertaining to distribution
of the software without specific, written prior permission.
LANCE ELLINGHOUSE DISCLAIMS ALL WARRANTIES WITH REGARD TO
THIS SOFTWARE, INCLUDING ALL IMPLIED WARRANTIES OF MERCHANTABILITY AND
FITNESS, IN NO EVENT SHALL LANCE ELLINGHOUSE CENTRUM BE LIABLE
FOR ANY SPECIAL, INDIRECT OR CONSEQUENTIAL DAMAGES OR ANY DAMAGES
WHATSOEVER RESULTING FROM LOSS OF USE, DATA OR PROFITS, WHETHER IN AN
ACTION OF CONTRACT, NEGLIGENCE OR OTHER TORTIOUS ACTION, ARISING OUT
OF OR IN CONNECTION WITH THE USE OR PERFORMANCE OF THIS SOFTWARE.

Modified by Jack Jansen, CWI, July 1995:
- Use binascii module to do the actual line-by-line conversion
  between ascii and binary. This results in a 1000-fold speedup. The C
  version is still 5 times faster, though.
- Arguments more compliant with Python standard
```

C.3.8 XML Remote Procedure Calls

The xmlrpc.client module contains the following notice:

```
    The XML-RPC client interface is

Copyright (c) 1999-2002 by Secret Labs AB
Copyright (c) 1999-2002 by Fredrik Lundh

By obtaining, using, and/or copying this software and/or its
associated documentation, you agree that you have read, understood,
and will comply with the following terms and conditions:

Permission to use, copy, modify, and distribute this software and
its associated documentation for any purpose and without fee is
hereby granted, provided that the above copyright notice appears in
```

all copies, and that both that copyright notice and this permission
notice appear in supporting documentation, and that the name of
Secret Labs AB or the author not be used in advertising or publicity
pertaining to distribution of the software without specific, written
prior permission.

SECRET LABS AB AND THE AUTHOR DISCLAIMS ALL WARRANTIES WITH REGARD
TO THIS SOFTWARE, INCLUDING ALL IMPLIED WARRANTIES OF MERCHANT-
ABILITY AND FITNESS. IN NO EVENT SHALL SECRET LABS AB OR THE AUTHOR
BE LIABLE FOR ANY SPECIAL, INDIRECT OR CONSEQUENTIAL DAMAGES OR ANY
DAMAGES WHATSOEVER RESULTING FROM LOSS OF USE, DATA OR PROFITS,
WHETHER IN AN ACTION OF CONTRACT, NEGLIGENCE OR OTHER TORTIOUS
ACTION, ARISING OUT OF OR IN CONNECTION WITH THE USE OR PERFORMANCE
OF THIS SOFTWARE.

C.3.9 test_epoll

The test_epoll contains the following notice:

Copyright (c) 2001-2006 Twisted Matrix Laboratories.

Permission is hereby granted, free of charge, to any person obtaining
a copy of this software and associated documentation files (the
"Software"), to deal in the Software without restriction, including
without limitation the rights to use, copy, modify, merge, publish,
distribute, sublicense, and/or sell copies of the Software, and to
permit persons to whom the Software is furnished to do so, subject to
the following conditions:

The above copyright notice and this permission notice shall be
included in all copies or substantial portions of the Software.

THE SOFTWARE IS PROVIDED "AS IS", WITHOUT WARRANTY OF ANY KIND,
EXPRESS OR IMPLIED, INCLUDING BUT NOT LIMITED TO THE WARRANTIES OF
MERCHANTABILITY, FITNESS FOR A PARTICULAR PURPOSE AND
NONINFRINGEMENT. IN NO EVENT SHALL THE AUTHORS OR COPYRIGHT HOLDERS BE
LIABLE FOR ANY CLAIM, DAMAGES OR OTHER LIABILITY, WHETHER IN AN ACTION
OF CONTRACT, TORT OR OTHERWISE, ARISING FROM, OUT OF OR IN CONNECTION
WITH THE SOFTWARE OR THE USE OR OTHER DEALINGS IN THE SOFTWARE.

C.3.10 Select kqueue

The select and contains the following notice for the kqueue interface:

Copyright (c) 2000 Doug White, 2006 James Knight, 2007 Christian Heimes
All rights reserved.

Redistribution and use in source and binary forms, with or without
modification, are permitted provided that the following conditions
are met:
1. Redistributions of source code must retain the above copyright
   notice, this list of conditions and the following disclaimer.
2. Redistributions in binary form must reproduce the above copyright

```
  notice, this list of conditions and the following disclaimer in the
  documentation and/or other materials provided with the distribution.

THIS SOFTWARE IS PROVIDED BY THE AUTHOR AND CONTRIBUTORS ``AS IS'' AND
ANY EXPRESS OR IMPLIED WARRANTIES, INCLUDING, BUT NOT LIMITED TO, THE
IMPLIED WARRANTIES OF MERCHANTABILITY AND FITNESS FOR A PARTICULAR PURPOSE
ARE DISCLAIMED.  IN NO EVENT SHALL THE AUTHOR OR CONTRIBUTORS BE LIABLE
FOR ANY DIRECT, INDIRECT, INCIDENTAL, SPECIAL, EXEMPLARY, OR CONSEQUENTIAL
DAMAGES (INCLUDING, BUT NOT LIMITED TO, PROCUREMENT OF SUBSTITUTE GOODS
OR SERVICES; LOSS OF USE, DATA, OR PROFITS; OR BUSINESS INTERRUPTION)
HOWEVER CAUSED AND ON ANY THEORY OF LIABILITY, WHETHER IN CONTRACT, STRICT
LIABILITY, OR TORT (INCLUDING NEGLIGENCE OR OTHERWISE) ARISING IN ANY WAY
OUT OF THE USE OF THIS SOFTWARE, EVEN IF ADVISED OF THE POSSIBILITY OF
SUCH DAMAGE.
```

C.3.11 SipHash24

The file `Python/pyhash.c` contains Marek Majkowski' implementation of Dan Bernstein's SipHash24 algorithm. The contains the following note:

```
<MIT License>
Copyright (c) 2013  Marek Majkowski <marek@popcount.org>

Permission is hereby granted, free of charge, to any person obtaining a copy
of this software and associated documentation files (the "Software"), to deal
in the Software without restriction, including without limitation the rights
to use, copy, modify, merge, publish, distribute, sublicense, and/or sell
copies of the Software, and to permit persons to whom the Software is
furnished to do so, subject to the following conditions:

The above copyright notice and this permission notice shall be included in
all copies or substantial portions of the Software.
</MIT License>

Original location:
   https://github.com/majek/csiphash/

Solution inspired by code from:
   Samuel Neves (supercop/crypto_auth/siphash24/little)
   djb (supercop/crypto_auth/siphash24/little2)
   Jean-Philippe Aumasson (https://131002.net/siphash/siphash24.c)
```

C.3.12 strtod and dtoa

The file `Python/dtoa.c`, which supplies C functions dtoa and strtod for conversion of C doubles to and from strings, is derived from the file of the same name by David M. Gay, currently available from http://www.netlib.org/fp/. The original file, as retrieved on March 16, 2009, contains the following copyright and licensing notice:

```
/*****************************************************************
 *
 * The author of this software is David M. Gay.
 *
 * Copyright (c) 1991, 2000, 2001 by Lucent Technologies.
```

```
*
* Permission to use, copy, modify, and distribute this software for any
* purpose without fee is hereby granted, provided that this entire notice
* is included in all copies of any software which is or includes a copy
* or modification of this software and in all copies of the supporting
* documentation for such software.
*
* THIS SOFTWARE IS BEING PROVIDED "AS IS", WITHOUT ANY EXPRESS OR IMPLIED
* WARRANTY.  IN PARTICULAR, NEITHER THE AUTHOR NOR LUCENT MAKES ANY
* REPRESENTATION OR WARRANTY OF ANY KIND CONCERNING THE MERCHANTABILITY
* OF THIS SOFTWARE OR ITS FITNESS FOR ANY PARTICULAR PURPOSE.
*
**************************************************************/
```

C.3.13 OpenSSL

The modules `hashlib`, `posix`, `ssl`, `crypt` use the OpenSSL library for added performance if made available by the operating system. Additionally, the Windows and Mac OS X installers for Python may include a copy of the OpenSSL libraries, so we include a copy of the OpenSSL license here:

```
LICENSE ISSUES
==============

The OpenSSL toolkit stays under a dual license, i.e. both the conditions of
the OpenSSL License and the original SSLeay license apply to the toolkit.
See below for the actual license texts. Actually both licenses are BSD-style
Open Source licenses. In case of any license issues related to OpenSSL
please contact openssl-core@openssl.org.

OpenSSL License
---------------
```

```
/* ====================================================================
 * Copyright (c) 1998-2008 The OpenSSL Project.  All rights reserved.
 *
 * Redistribution and use in source and binary forms, with or without
 * modification, are permitted provided that the following conditions
 * are met:
 *
 * 1. Redistributions of source code must retain the above copyright
 *    notice, this list of conditions and the following disclaimer.
 *
 * 2. Redistributions in binary form must reproduce the above copyright
 *    notice, this list of conditions and the following disclaimer in
 *    the documentation and/or other materials provided with the
 *    distribution.
 *
 * 3. All advertising materials mentioning features or use of this
 *    software must display the following acknowledgment:
 *    "This product includes software developed by the OpenSSL Project
 *    for use in the OpenSSL Toolkit. (http://www.openssl.org/)"
 *
 * 4. The names "OpenSSL Toolkit" and "OpenSSL Project" must not be used to
 *    endorse or promote products derived from this software without
```

```
 *    prior written permission. For written permission, please contact
 *    openssl-core@openssl.org.
 *
 * 5. Products derived from this software may not be called "OpenSSL"
 *    nor may "OpenSSL" appear in their names without prior written
 *    permission of the OpenSSL Project.
 *
 * 6. Redistributions of any form whatsoever must retain the following
 *    acknowledgment:
 *    "This product includes software developed by the OpenSSL Project
 *    for use in the OpenSSL Toolkit (http://www.openssl.org/)"
 *
 * THIS SOFTWARE IS PROVIDED BY THE OpenSSL PROJECT ``AS IS'' AND ANY
 * EXPRESSED OR IMPLIED WARRANTIES, INCLUDING, BUT NOT LIMITED TO, THE
 * IMPLIED WARRANTIES OF MERCHANTABILITY AND FITNESS FOR A PARTICULAR
 * PURPOSE ARE DISCLAIMED.  IN NO EVENT SHALL THE OpenSSL PROJECT OR
 * ITS CONTRIBUTORS BE LIABLE FOR ANY DIRECT, INDIRECT, INCIDENTAL,
 * SPECIAL, EXEMPLARY, OR CONSEQUENTIAL DAMAGES (INCLUDING, BUT
 * NOT LIMITED TO, PROCUREMENT OF SUBSTITUTE GOODS OR SERVICES;
 * LOSS OF USE, DATA, OR PROFITS; OR BUSINESS INTERRUPTION)
 * HOWEVER CAUSED AND ON ANY THEORY OF LIABILITY, WHETHER IN CONTRACT,
 * STRICT LIABILITY, OR TORT (INCLUDING NEGLIGENCE OR OTHERWISE)
 * ARISING IN ANY WAY OUT OF THE USE OF THIS SOFTWARE, EVEN IF ADVISED
 * OF THE POSSIBILITY OF SUCH DAMAGE.
 * ======================================================================
 *
 * This product includes cryptographic software written by Eric Young
 * (eay@cryptsoft.com).  This product includes software written by Tim
 * Hudson (tjh@cryptsoft.com).
 *
 */
```

```
Original SSLeay License
-----------------------
```

```
 /* Copyright (C) 1995-1998 Eric Young (eay@cryptsoft.com)
 * All rights reserved.
 *
 * This package is an SSL implementation written
 * by Eric Young (eay@cryptsoft.com).
 * The implementation was written so as to conform with Netscapes SSL.
 *
 * This library is free for commercial and non-commercial use as long as
 * the following conditions are aheared to.  The following conditions
 * apply to all code found in this distribution, be it the RC4, RSA,
 * lhash, DES, etc., code; not just the SSL code.  The SSL documentation
 * included with this distribution is covered by the same copyright terms
 * except that the holder is Tim Hudson (tjh@cryptsoft.com).
 *
 * Copyright remains Eric Young's, and as such any Copyright notices in
 * the code are not to be removed.
 * If this package is used in a product, Eric Young should be given attribution
 * as the author of the parts of the library used.
 * This can be in the form of a textual message at program startup or
```

```
 *   in documentation (online or textual) provided with the package.
 *
 *   Redistribution and use in source and binary forms, with or without
 *   modification, are permitted provided that the following conditions
 *   are met:
 *   1. Redistributions of source code must retain the copyright
 *      notice, this list of conditions and the following disclaimer.
 *   2. Redistributions in binary form must reproduce the above copyright
 *      notice, this list of conditions and the following disclaimer in the
 *      documentation and/or other materials provided with the distribution.
 *   3. All advertising materials mentioning features or use of this software
 *      must display the following acknowledgement:
 *      "This product includes cryptographic software written by
 *       Eric Young (eay@cryptsoft.com)"
 *      The word 'cryptographic' can be left out if the rouines from the library
 *      being used are not cryptographic related :-).
 *   4. If you include any Windows specific code (or a derivative thereof) from
 *      the apps directory (application code) you must include an acknowledgement:
 *      "This product includes software written by Tim Hudson (tjh@cryptsoft.com)"
 *
 *   THIS SOFTWARE IS PROVIDED BY ERIC YOUNG ``AS IS'' AND
 *   ANY EXPRESS OR IMPLIED WARRANTIES, INCLUDING, BUT NOT LIMITED TO, THE
 *   IMPLIED WARRANTIES OF MERCHANTABILITY AND FITNESS FOR A PARTICULAR PURPOSE
 *   ARE DISCLAIMED.  IN NO EVENT SHALL THE AUTHOR OR CONTRIBUTORS BE LIABLE
 *   FOR ANY DIRECT, INDIRECT, INCIDENTAL, SPECIAL, EXEMPLARY, OR CONSEQUENTIAL
 *   DAMAGES (INCLUDING, BUT NOT LIMITED TO, PROCUREMENT OF SUBSTITUTE GOODS
 *   OR SERVICES; LOSS OF USE, DATA, OR PROFITS; OR BUSINESS INTERRUPTION)
 *   HOWEVER CAUSED AND ON ANY THEORY OF LIABILITY, WHETHER IN CONTRACT, STRICT
 *   LIABILITY, OR TORT (INCLUDING NEGLIGENCE OR OTHERWISE) ARISING IN ANY WAY
 *   OUT OF THE USE OF THIS SOFTWARE, EVEN IF ADVISED OF THE POSSIBILITY OF
 *   SUCH DAMAGE.
 *
 *   The licence and distribution terms for any publically available version or
 *   derivative of this code cannot be changed.  i.e. this code cannot simply be
 *   copied and put under another distribution licence
 *   [including the GNU Public Licence.]
 */
```

C.3.14 expat

The pyexpat extension is built using an included copy of the expat sources unless the build is configured --with-system-expat:

```
Copyright (c) 1998, 1999, 2000 Thai Open Source Software Center Ltd
                        and Clark Cooper

Permission is hereby granted, free of charge, to any person obtaining
a copy of this software and associated documentation files (the
"Software"), to deal in the Software without restriction, including
without limitation the rights to use, copy, modify, merge, publish,
distribute, sublicense, and/or sell copies of the Software, and to
permit persons to whom the Software is furnished to do so, subject to
the following conditions:
```

The above copyright notice and this permission notice shall be included
in all copies or substantial portions of the Software.

THE SOFTWARE IS PROVIDED "AS IS", WITHOUT WARRANTY OF ANY KIND,
EXPRESS OR IMPLIED, INCLUDING BUT NOT LIMITED TO THE WARRANTIES OF
MERCHANTABILITY, FITNESS FOR A PARTICULAR PURPOSE AND NONINFRINGEMENT.
IN NO EVENT SHALL THE AUTHORS OR COPYRIGHT HOLDERS BE LIABLE FOR ANY
CLAIM, DAMAGES OR OTHER LIABILITY, WHETHER IN AN ACTION OF CONTRACT,
TORT OR OTHERWISE, ARISING FROM, OUT OF OR IN CONNECTION WITH THE
SOFTWARE OR THE USE OR OTHER DEALINGS IN THE SOFTWARE.

C.3.15 libffi

The _ctypes extension is built using an included copy of the libffi sources unless the build is configured
--with-system-libffi:

Copyright (c) 1996-2008 Red Hat, Inc and others.

Permission is hereby granted, free of charge, to any person obtaining
a copy of this software and associated documentation files (the
``Software''), to deal in the Software without restriction, including
without limitation the rights to use, copy, modify, merge, publish,
distribute, sublicense, and/or sell copies of the Software, and to
permit persons to whom the Software is furnished to do so, subject to
the following conditions:

The above copyright notice and this permission notice shall be included
in all copies or substantial portions of the Software.

THE SOFTWARE IS PROVIDED ``AS IS'', WITHOUT WARRANTY OF ANY KIND,
EXPRESS OR IMPLIED, INCLUDING BUT NOT LIMITED TO THE WARRANTIES OF
MERCHANTABILITY, FITNESS FOR A PARTICULAR PURPOSE AND
NONINFRINGEMENT. IN NO EVENT SHALL THE AUTHORS OR COPYRIGHT
HOLDERS BE LIABLE FOR ANY CLAIM, DAMAGES OR OTHER LIABILITY,
WHETHER IN AN ACTION OF CONTRACT, TORT OR OTHERWISE, ARISING FROM,
OUT OF OR IN CONNECTION WITH THE SOFTWARE OR THE USE OR OTHER
DEALINGS IN THE SOFTWARE.

C.3.16 zlib

The zlib extension is built using an included copy of the zlib sources if the zlib version found on the system is too
old to be used for the build:

Copyright (C) 1995-2011 Jean-loup Gailly and Mark Adler

This software is provided 'as-is', without any express or implied
warranty. In no event will the authors be held liable for any damages
arising from the use of this software.

Permission is granted to anyone to use this software for any purpose,
including commercial applications, and to alter it and redistribute it
freely, subject to the following restrictions:

1. The origin of this software must not be misrepresented; you must not claim that you wrote the original software. If you use this software in a product, an acknowledgment in the product documentation would be appreciated but is not required.

2. Altered source versions must be plainly marked as such, and must not be misrepresented as being the original software.

3. This notice may not be removed or altered from any source distribution.

```
Jean-loup Gailly        Mark Adler
jloup@gzip.org          madler@alumni.caltech.edu
```

C.3.17 cfuhash

The implementation of the hash table used by the `tracemalloc` is based on the cfuhash project:

```
Copyright (c) 2005 Don Owens
All rights reserved.

This code is released under the BSD license:

Redistribution and use in source and binary forms, with or without
modification, are permitted provided that the following conditions
are met:
```

* Redistributions of source code must retain the above copyright notice, this list of conditions and the following disclaimer.

* Redistributions in binary form must reproduce the above copyright notice, this list of conditions and the following disclaimer in the documentation and/or other materials provided with the distribution.

* Neither the name of the author nor the names of its contributors may be used to endorse or promote products derived from this software without specific prior written permission.

```
THIS SOFTWARE IS PROVIDED BY THE COPYRIGHT HOLDERS AND CONTRIBUTORS
"AS IS" AND ANY EXPRESS OR IMPLIED WARRANTIES, INCLUDING, BUT NOT
LIMITED TO, THE IMPLIED WARRANTIES OF MERCHANTABILITY AND FITNESS
FOR A PARTICULAR PURPOSE ARE DISCLAIMED. IN NO EVENT SHALL THE
COPYRIGHT OWNER OR CONTRIBUTORS BE LIABLE FOR ANY DIRECT, INDIRECT,
INCIDENTAL, SPECIAL, EXEMPLARY, OR CONSEQUENTIAL DAMAGES
(INCLUDING, BUT NOT LIMITED TO, PROCUREMENT OF SUBSTITUTE GOODS OR
SERVICES; LOSS OF USE, DATA, OR PROFITS; OR BUSINESS INTERRUPTION)
HOWEVER CAUSED AND ON ANY THEORY OF LIABILITY, WHETHER IN CONTRACT,
STRICT LIABILITY, OR TORT (INCLUDING NEGLIGENCE OR OTHERWISE)
ARISING IN ANY WAY OUT OF THE USE OF THIS SOFTWARE, EVEN IF ADVISED
OF THE POSSIBILITY OF SUCH DAMAGE.
```

C.3.18 libmpdec

The _decimal Module is built using an included copy of the libmpdec library unless the build is configured --with-system-libmpdec:

```
Copyright (c) 2008-2016 Stefan Krah. All rights reserved.

Redistribution and use in source and binary forms, with or without
modification, are permitted provided that the following conditions
are met:

1. Redistributions of source code must retain the above copyright
   notice, this list of conditions and the following disclaimer.

2. Redistributions in binary form must reproduce the above copyright
   notice, this list of conditions and the following disclaimer in the
   documentation and/or other materials provided with the distribution.

THIS SOFTWARE IS PROVIDED BY THE AUTHOR AND CONTRIBUTORS "AS IS" AND
ANY EXPRESS OR IMPLIED WARRANTIES, INCLUDING, BUT NOT LIMITED TO, THE
IMPLIED WARRANTIES OF MERCHANTABILITY AND FITNESS FOR A PARTICULAR PURPOSE
ARE DISCLAIMED.  IN NO EVENT SHALL THE AUTHOR OR CONTRIBUTORS BE LIABLE
FOR ANY DIRECT, INDIRECT, INCIDENTAL, SPECIAL, EXEMPLARY, OR CONSEQUENTIAL
DAMAGES (INCLUDING, BUT NOT LIMITED TO, PROCUREMENT OF SUBSTITUTE GOODS
OR SERVICES; LOSS OF USE, DATA, OR PROFITS; OR BUSINESS INTERRUPTION)
HOWEVER CAUSED AND ON ANY THEORY OF LIABILITY, WHETHER IN CONTRACT, STRICT
LIABILITY, OR TORT (INCLUDING NEGLIGENCE OR OTHERWISE) ARISING IN ANY WAY
OUT OF THE USE OF THIS SOFTWARE, EVEN IF ADVISED OF THE POSSIBILITY OF
SUCH DAMAGE.
```

COPYRIGHT

Python and this documentation is:

See *History and License* for complete license and permissions information.

Symbols

A

B

C